OUR BEST CUPCAKES,
COOKIES, CANDY AND MORE

BY THE EDITORS OF **FOOD NETWORK MAGAZINE**

CLARKSON POTTER/PUBLISHERS
NEW YORK

Published in the United States by Clarkson Potter/Publishers, an imprint of the Crown Publishing Group, a division of Random House, Inc., New York.
www.crownpublishing.com
www.clarksonpotter.com

CLARKSON POTTER is a trademark and POTTER with colophon is a registered trademark of Random House, Inc.

Recipes and photographs originally appeared in issues of *Food Network Magazine*.

Library of Congress Cataloging-in-Publication Data
Sweet : our best cupcakes, cookies, candy, and more /
editors of Food Network Magazine. -- First edition.
Includes index.
1. Desserts. I. Food Network (Firm) II. Food network magazine.
TX773.S9894 2014
641.86—dc23 2013032510

A complete list of photography credits appears on page 336.

ISBN 978-0-8041-3768-3
eBook ISBN 978-0-8041-3769-0

Printed in China

Book and cover design by Ashley Tucker

10 9 8 7 6 5 4 3 2

First Edition

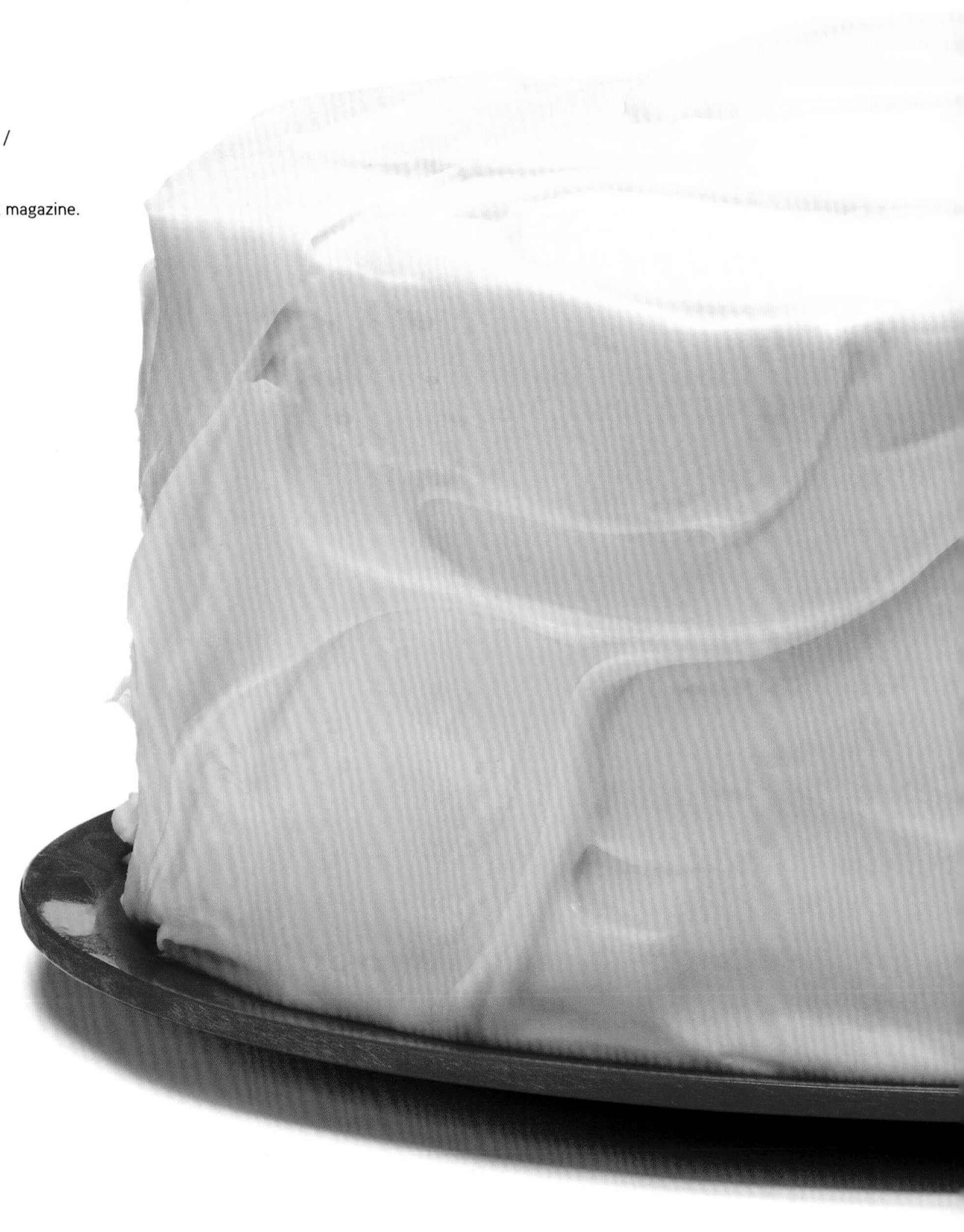

TO YOU...
AND YOUR SWEET TOOTH

acknowledgments

This book is the result of countless hours of recipe development and testing by the incredible team in Food Network Kitchens. Thanks, especially, to Food Network's culinary leader, Katherine Alford, who has a never-ending supply of fantastic ideas.

Enormous thanks to our food director, Liz Sgroi, for leading this project and for contributing in too many ways to name. Thanks to our managing editor, Maria Baugh, who kept us all on task; to our copy editor, Joy Sanchez; and to Ellery Badcock for organizing the massive recipe collection. Thanks to the Hearst Books team: Jacqueline Deval, vice president, publisher; and Mark Gompertz, creative director, content extensions, who introduced us to our great partners at Clarkson Potter, Publisher Pam Krauss, Associate Publisher Doris Cooper, Senior Editor Emily Takoudes, Creative Director Marysarah Quinn, Art Director Jane Treuhaft and Designer Ashley Tucker.

We can't say enough to thank Creative Director Deirdre Koribanick. She brings so much energy to the pages of the magazine, and she has done the same in this book. Thanks to Photo Director Alice Albert and her team for producing the spectacular images: We love seeing them come to life in new form. Thanks to Casey Oto for sourcing every photo, and to Ian Doherty, Robert Valin and Lydia Paniccia for getting every page in perfect shape.

We are ever grateful for the strong partnership that led to *Food Network Magazine*. Thanks to Food Network President Brooke Bailey Johnson; General Manager, Scripps Enterprises Sergei Kuharsky; and at Hearst, President David Carey; President, Marketing and Publishing Director Michael Clinton; Executive Vice President and General Manager John P. Loughlin; and especially to our mentor, Editorial Director Ellen Levine.

CONTENTS

Cupcakes & Whoopie Pies

22 Peanut Brittle Chocolate Cupcakes

25 Chocolate Egg Cream Cupcakes

26 Strawberry Surprise Cupcakes

29 Low-Fat Chocolate Cupcakes

30 Chocolate Malt Cupcakes

33 Tea Cakes with Earl Grey Icing

34 Mint Patty Cakes

37 Mini Carrot Cupcakes

38 Mini Peanut Butter–Chocolate Cupcakes

41 Cherry-Pistachio Tea Cakes

42 Vanilla Cupcakes with Swiss Meringue Frosting

45 Chocolate and Olive Oil Fig Cakes

46 Coconut Cupcakes with Chocolate and Almonds

49 Mini Bacon Cheesecakes

50 Cranberry Cupcakes

52 Seven Twists on Whoopie Pies

55 Blueberry-Lemon Whoopie Pies

56 Red Velvet Whoopie Pies

58 Alphabet Cupcakes

Cookies & Bars

63 Lemon–White Chocolate Cookies

64 Salted Caramel–Pretzel Thumbprints

67 Chewy Chocolate Chip Cookies

68 Almond Corn Puff Cookies

71 Chewy Oatmeal-Raisin Cookies

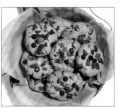

72 Peanut Butter–Bacon Cookies

75 Nutty Sandwich Cookies

76 Peanut Butter–Jam Macaroons

78 Pistachio Macaroons

79 Cinnamon Pinwheels

80 Four Twists on Brownies

82 Strawberry Blondies

85 Classic Lemon Bars

86 Salted Pretzel–Marshmallow Bars

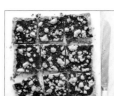

89 Jam Shortbread

90 PB&J Chocolate Bars

92 Chocolate Chip Shortbread

93 Cookie Puzzle

Candy & Snacks

96 Mini Toasted Strawberry Shortcakes

97 Fruit Jellies

98 Cinnamon Raisin–Nut Toffee

100 Four Twists on Chocolate Bark

103 Chocolate Truffles

104 Chocolate Fudge

106 Sea Salt Chocolate Caramels

107 Honeycomb Candy

109 Apple Cider Doughnuts

110 Rainbow Petits Fours

113 Watermelon-Lime Gelatin Squares

114 Grape Jelly Breakfast Tarts

117 Churros with Coconut Sauce

118 Grilled Pineapple Upside-Down Cakes

119 Coconut-Almond Popcorn Balls

121 Cereal Brittle

122 Fruit Leather Roll-Ups

125 Cone-oli

126 Chocolate-Dipped Treats

Pies & Crumbles

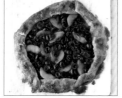

Fake-Out Cakes

174 Pencil Cake

176 Caramel Apple Cake

178 Strawberry Pie Cake

180 Carrot Cake

182 Peanut Butter and Jelly Sandwich Cake

184 Tiki Cocktail Cake

186 Cheeseburger Cake

188 Steak Frites Cake

190 Spaghetti and Meatballs Cake

192 Candy Bar Cake

194 Cheese Wheel Cake

196 Flowerpot Cake

198 Guacamole and Chips Cake

200 Popcorn Cake

202 Lobster Roll Cake

Show-Off Cakes

 **206** Boston Cream Pie

 **209** Bourbon Praline Cake

 **210** Lemon-Cranberry Bundt Cake

 **213** Caramel Apple Upside-Down Cake

 **214** Blueberry Buttermilk Bundt Cake

 **217** Coconut Roulade with Rum Buttercream

 **218** Dulce de Leche Crêpe Cake

 **221** Strawberry Shortcake Layer Cake

 **222** S'mores Cake

 **225** Towering Flourless Chocolate Cake

 **226** Red Velvet Layer Cake

 **229** Hummingbird Cake

 **230** Almond Layer Cake with White Chocolate Frosting

 **233** Hazelnut Dacquoise

 **234** Three Twists on Vanilla Cake

 **237** Three-Layer Carrot Cake

 **238** Peppermint Layer Cake with Candy Cane Frosting

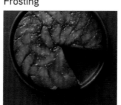 **241** Salted Caramel–Orange Upside-Down Cake

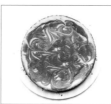 **242** Red Velvet Cheesecake

 **245** Rocky Road Cheesecake

 **246** White Chocolate–Cranberry Cheesecake

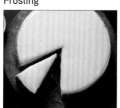 **249** Cheesecake with Lemon–Ginger Curd

 **250** Color Your Frosting

Frozen Treats

254 Peach Cobbler Ice Cream Cake

257 Neapolitan Ice Cream Cake

258 Toasted Marshmallow Ice Cream Cake

261 Ice Cream Crunch Cake

262 Lemon-Raspberry Sorbet Cake

265 Salted Caramel Ice Cream Cone Cake

266 Baked Alaska

269 Vanilla Malted Ice Cream Cake

270 Chocolate-Banana Ice Cream Pie

273 Coffee-Coconut Ice Cream Bombe

274 Five Twists on Ice Cream Sandwiches

277 Chocolate-Hazelnut Ice Cream Cupcakes

278 Samoa Tartlets

281 Cherry-Chocolate Ice Cream

282 Ice Cream Sundae Cones

285 Mini Ice Cream Sandwich Cakes

286 Orange Cream Pops

288 Italian Ice

289 Chocolate Bowls

Holiday Desserts

292 Conversation Hearts

295 Chocolate Birds' Nests

296 King Cake

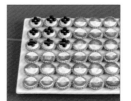
299 Fruit-Tart Flag

300 Star-Studded Berry Tarts

303 Ghastly Meringues

304 Candy Bucket Cake

306 Six Twists on Caramel Apples

308 Candy Corn Cake

311 Polka-Dot Pumpkin Pie

312 Holiday Sugar Cookies

315 Peppermint Croquembouche

316 Candy Cane Pavlova

319 Gingerbread People

322 Hot Cocoa Cookies

325 Cocoa Thumbprints

326 German Chocolate Yule Log

328 Edible Trees

introduction

We were wrapping up a photo shoot for *Food Network Magazine*'s Piece of Cake column a while back, and our deputy art director, Marc Davila, said he wanted to take the cake we'd shot to a party that night. If you've seen the column, you know that these aren't ordinary cakes—they're full-on spectacles: a giant burger, an oversize caramel apple, an ice cream steak with pound cake fries. The cake that Marc planned to take was the one pictured here (see page 194 for the how-to). When he showed up at the party, his friends were beyond happy. They told him no one had brought cheese and they desperately needed some—how awesome that he had come with a whole wheel! Since then, our food director, Liz Sgroi, has conceived of many other incredible look-alikes, including "guacamole" made of green ice cream in a chocolate-cake molcajete (stone bowl) and a lobster-roll cake made of a split pound cake with ambrosia-like filling.

These fake-out cakes are only a small part of our dessert collection, but when we sat down to put this book together we realized that all the sweets in the magazine have something in common: They're fun, not frilly. To be honest, they're desserts that any 5-year-old would love: a cake covered with ice cream cones (page 265), a toasted-marshmallow pie (page 134), macaroons that taste like a PB&J (page 76). Don't get me wrong: We take desserts seriously around here—we just don't think they need to be overly complicated.

You'll see as you flip through that the chefs in Food Network Kitchens don't use crazy pans or ingredients you can't find, and they don't break out a piping bag very often, either. One of the test kitchen's best dessert ideas of all time is an ice cream sandwich made with nothing but caramel sauce, vanilla ice cream and Ritz crackers. I threw some together for a Fourth of July party instead of my usual elaborate ice cream cake roll, and everyone went nuts. I will now save at least an hour and a half on dessert prep at future summer parties by making these. In other words, they changed my life. I hope you find something in this book that does the same for you.

Maile Carpenter
Editor in Chief

PEANUT BRITTLE CHOCOLATE CUPCAKES

MAKES 24 CUPCAKES

ACTIVE: 1 hr 10 min

TOTAL: 1 hr 50 min

FOR THE CUPCAKES

- 3 sticks unsalted butter, cut into pieces
- 1 cup unsweetened Dutch-process cocoa powder
- 3¼ cups packed dark brown sugar
- 3 cups all-purpose flour
- 1 teaspoon baking powder
- ½ teaspoon baking soda
- ¾ teaspoon salt
- 1¼ cups buttermilk
- 2 large eggs, at room temperature
- 2 teaspoons vanilla extract

FOR THE BRITTLE

- ½ cup granulated sugar
- ¼ cup creamy peanut butter
- ¼ cup butterscotch chips

FOR THE FROSTING

- 1 cup heavy cream
- 2 10-ounce bags peanut butter chips

If you don't have buttermilk on hand for these, just use ¾ cup whole milk and ½ cup plain yogurt or sour cream.

1 Make the cupcakes: Preheat the oven to 350°. Line two 12-cup muffin pans with paper liners. Put the butter, cocoa powder and ¾ cup water in a microwave-safe bowl, cover with plastic wrap and microwave until the butter melts, about 2 minutes. Whisk to combine, then whisk in the brown sugar.

2 Whisk the flour, baking powder, baking soda and salt in a large bowl. Whisk in the warm cocoa mixture. In another bowl, beat the buttermilk, eggs and vanilla; stir into the batter until just combined (don't overmix).

3 Divide the batter among the prepared muffin cups, filling each cup three-quarters of the way. Bake until the cupcakes are slightly domed and spring back when lightly pressed, about 30 minutes. Let cool in the pans 10 minutes, then transfer to racks to cool completely.

4 Make the brittle: Line a baking sheet with a silicone mat or parchment paper. Place the granulated sugar in a small saucepan over medium-high heat, bring to a boil and cook, swirling the pan but not stirring, until it turns amber. Remove from the heat; stir in the peanut butter and butterscotch chips until smooth. Immediately pour the mixture onto the prepared baking sheet, smooth into a thin layer with a spatula and let cool. Break the brittle into large pieces, place in a resealable plastic bag and crush with a rolling pin.

5 Make the frosting: Bring the cream to a simmer in a small saucepan. Remove from the heat, add the peanut butter chips and let stand about 5 minutes. Whisk until smooth. Place the pan over a bowl of ice, stirring occasionally, until the frosting is spreadable, about 10 minutes. Spread on the cupcakes or transfer to a pastry bag with a large round tip and pipe on top; sprinkle with the brittle.

CHOCOLATE EGG CREAM CUPCAKES

MAKES 6 CUPCAKES

ACTIVE: 50 min
TOTAL: 1 hr 20 min

FOR THE CUPCAKES

¼ cup unsweetened cocoa powder
¼ cup chocolate syrup
⅔ cup all-purpose flour
⅓ cup granulated sugar
¼ teaspoon baking soda
¼ teaspoon baking powder
¼ teaspoon salt
¼ cup vegetable oil
1 large egg
2 tablespoons whole milk
½ teaspoon vanilla extract

FOR THE FROSTING

1 ounce milk chocolate
6 tablespoons unsalted butter, at room temperature
½ teaspoon vanilla extract
2 cups confectioners' sugar
¼ cup whole milk
2 tablespoons unsweetened cocoa powder
2 pinches of salt
2 tablespoons malted milk powder
Pretzel rods, for topping

Try this fun frosting trick: Put two different kinds of frosting in separate disposable pastry bags, then position both bags in a larger pastry bag fitted with a star tip. When you pipe, the frosting will come out swirled!

1 Make the cupcakes: Preheat the oven to 350°. Line a 6-cup muffin pan with paper liners. Whisk the cocoa powder with ⅓ cup hot water in a medium bowl until dissolved. Whisk in the chocolate syrup until smooth; let cool slightly. In a large bowl, whisk the flour, granulated sugar, baking soda, baking powder and salt.

2 Whisk the vegetable oil, egg, milk and vanilla into the cocoa mixture until smooth, then fold into the flour mixture until just combined. Divide among the prepared muffin cups. Bake until a toothpick comes out clean, 18 to 20 minutes. Let cool 10 minutes in the pan, then remove to a rack to cool completely.

3 Make the frosting: Chop the chocolate and place in a microwave-safe bowl; microwave on 70% power in 30-second intervals, stirring, until melted. Let cool slightly. Cut the butter into pieces; beat the butter, vanilla and confectioners' sugar in a bowl with a mixer on medium-high speed until fluffy. Add 3 tablespoons milk and beat until smooth, 3 minutes. Remove half of the frosting to a separate bowl; add the cocoa powder, melted chocolate and a pinch of salt and beat until fluffy, 2 minutes. Mix the remaining 1 tablespoon milk and the malted milk powder in a cup, then add to the plain frosting; add a pinch of salt and beat until fluffy, about 2 minutes. If the frosting is too soft, cover and refrigerate until firm enough to pipe.

4 Put the 2 frostings in separate pastry bags and snip off the tips (or put in separate zip-top bags and snip off a corner of each). Position the frosting bags side by side in a large pastry bag fitted with a large star tip. Pipe the frosting onto the cupcakes in a spiral motion to create a swirl. Top with pretzel rods.

STRAWBERRY SURPRISE CUPCAKES

MAKES 6 CUPCAKES

ACTIVE: 30 min

TOTAL: 1 hr 20 min

FOR THE CUPCAKES

- 1½ cups all-purpose flour
- 1½ teaspoons baking powder
- ½ teaspoon salt
- 1 stick unsalted butter, at room temperature
- ¾ cup granulated sugar
- 2 large eggs, at room temperature
- 1 teaspoon vanilla extract
- ½ cup strawberry-flavored milk, at room temperature
- 6 strawberries, hulled

FOR THE FROSTING

- 2 cups confectioners' sugar
- ½ cup unsweetened cocoa powder
- 1 stick unsalted butter, at room temperature
- ½ cup heavy cream
- 3 strawberries, hulled and halved lengthwise

Stuff each of these cupcakes with a strawberry after baking, then hide it with frosting. When you slice the cupcakes in half, the strawberries look like hearts!

1 Make the cupcakes: Preheat the oven to 350°. Line a 6-cup jumbo muffin pan with paper liners. Whisk the flour, baking powder and salt in a medium bowl.

2 Beat the butter and granulated sugar in a large bowl with a mixer on medium-high speed until light and fluffy, about 3 minutes. Beat in the eggs, one at a time, then beat in the vanilla. Reduce the mixer speed to low; beat in the flour mixture in 3 batches, alternating with the strawberry milk, beginning and ending with flour, until just combined.

3 Divide the batter evenly among the prepared muffin cups. Bake until a toothpick inserted into a cupcake comes out clean, 25 to 30 minutes. Let cool 5 minutes in the pan, then remove to a rack to cool completely.

4 Using a paring knife, cut a cone-shaped piece of cake out of the top of each cupcake (about the same size as the strawberries), stopping about ½ inch from the bottom. Stuff each cupcake with 1 strawberry, then cover with a small piece of the removed cake.

5 Make the frosting: Sift the confectioners' sugar and cocoa powder into a medium bowl. Transfer half of the sugar-cocoa mixture to a large bowl; add the butter and ¼ cup cream and beat with a mixer on medium-high speed until smooth. Add the remaining sugar-cocoa mixture and ¼ cup cream and beat until fluffy. Transfer to a pastry bag fitted with a star tip and pipe onto the cupcakes. Top each with a strawberry half.

LOW-FAT CHOCOLATE CUPCAKES

MAKES 12 CUPCAKES

ACTIVE: 20 min
TOTAL: 50 min

FOR THE CUPCAKES
Cooking spray
½ cup pitted prunes
1 cup all-purpose flour
⅓ cup whole-wheat flour
⅓ cup unsweetened cocoa powder
1 teaspoon baking powder
¼ teaspoon baking soda
½ teaspoon salt
¼ teaspoon ground cinnamon
½ cup packed light brown sugar
2 large eggs
½ cup plain Greek yogurt
½ cup vegetable oil
1 teaspoon vanilla extract

FOR THE FROSTING
3 large egg whites
⅓ cup granulated sugar
⅛ teaspoon cream of tartar
Pinch of salt
2 tablespoons unsweetened cocoa powder
¼ teaspoon vanilla extract

You'd never know it, but we used prunes to make these cupcakes extra moist. To make mini cupcakes, bake in two 24-cup mini muffin pans for 12 to 14 minutes.

1 Make the cupcakes: Preheat the oven to 350°. Line a 12-cup muffin pan with paper liners; lightly spray the liners with cooking spray. Soak the prunes in a bowl with ¾ cup hot water until softened, about 10 minutes. Pour into a blender and puree until smooth.

2 Whisk the all-purpose flour, whole-wheat flour, cocoa powder, baking powder, baking soda, salt and cinnamon in a large bowl. In another bowl, whisk the prune puree, brown sugar, eggs, yogurt, vegetable oil and vanilla. Fold the wet ingredients into the dry ingredients until just combined (it's fine if there are a few lumps).

3 Divide the batter among the muffin cups, filling each cup three-quarters of the way. Bake until a toothpick comes out clean, 18 to 20 minutes. Transfer to a rack and let cool in the pan 10 minutes, then remove from the pan to cool completely.

4 Make the frosting: Whisk the egg whites, granulated sugar, cream of tartar and salt in a heatproof bowl set over a saucepan of simmering water until the sugar dissolves, 1 to 2 minutes (do not let the bowl touch the water). Remove the bowl from the pan. Transfer the egg white mixture to a stand mixer fitted with the whisk attachment; beat on medium-high speed until stiff peaks form, 3 to 5 minutes. Sift in the cocoa powder and add the vanilla; beat to combine. Spread the frosting on the cupcakes.

CHOCOLATE MALT CUPCAKES

MAKES 24 CUPCAKES

ACTIVE: 55 min

TOTAL: 1 hr 20 min (plus chilling)

FOR THE FROSTING

- ⅔ cup sugar
- 1 teaspoon light corn syrup
- 3 cups heavy cream
- 3 tablespoons unsalted butter
- 7 ounces milk chocolate, chopped
- 4 ounces bittersweet chocolate, chopped
- ½ teaspoon kosher salt

FOR THE CUPCAKES

- 2 cups all-purpose flour
- 1 tablespoon baking powder
- ¾ teaspoon fine salt
- 1 cup malted milk powder
- ¾ cup unsweetened Dutch-process cocoa powder
- 1⅓ cups sugar
- 1 stick unsalted butter, at room temperature
- 4 large eggs, at room temperature
- 1¾ cups half-and-half
- 1½ cups crispy rice cereal

You can make these cupcakes up to a week ahead and freeze in large resealable plastic bags. Then just thaw at room temperature and frost the day you need them.

1 Make the frosting: Sprinkle the sugar evenly in a large skillet and add the corn syrup. Bring to a boil over medium heat, stirring once or twice. Continue to boil, swirling the pan but not stirring, until the caramel is amber. Carefully pour in the heavy cream (it can splatter) and add the butter. Simmer, whisking constantly, until the caramel is smooth, about 2 minutes.

2 Combine both chocolates and the kosher salt in a medium heatproof bowl. Pour the hot caramel over the chocolate and let stand until melted, about 5 minutes. Whisk until smooth and shiny, then cover and refrigerate until set, at least 4 hours or overnight. (The frosting can be made up to 2 days ahead.)

3 Make the cupcakes: Preheat the oven to 375°. Line two 12-cup muffin pans with paper liners. Whisk the flour, baking powder and fine salt in a bowl. Sift the malted milk and cocoa powders into another bowl.

4 Beat the sugar and butter in a third bowl with a mixer until light and fluffy, about 7 minutes. Add the malted milk powder mixture; beat until combined. Add the eggs, one at a time, beating well after each addition. With the mixer on low speed, add the flour mixture in 3 batches, alternating with the half-and-half in 2 batches.

5 Divide the batter evenly among the prepared muffin cups, filling each cup about three-quarters of the way. Bake until a toothpick inserted into a cupcake comes out clean, 15 to 20 minutes. Let cool in the pans 10 minutes, then transfer to racks to cool completely.

6 Beat the chilled frosting with a mixer or whisk until thick, about 2 minutes (don't overwhip). Spread on the cupcakes or transfer to a pastry bag with a star tip and pipe on top. Refrigerate until ready to serve, then sprinkle with the cereal.

TEA CAKES WITH EARL GREY ICING

MAKES 48 TEA CAKES

ACTIVE: 55 min

TOTAL: 1 hr 10 min

FOR THE TEA CAKES

6 ounces bittersweet chocolate, chopped

2 sticks unsalted butter, cut into pieces

1½ cups sugar

¾ cup cake flour

½ teaspoon salt

4 large eggs

½ teaspoon vanilla extract

FOR THE ICING

1 cup sugar

4 large egg whites

1 teaspoon fresh lemon juice

Pinch of salt

2 bags Earl Grey tea

These bite-size cakes make a great gift for a tea-lover. Package them with a canister of loose tea and a mug.

1 Make the tea cakes: Preheat the oven to 350°. Line two 24-cup mini-muffin pans with paper liners. Melt the chocolate and butter in a heatproof bowl set over a saucepan of simmering water (do not let the bowl touch the water). Whisk until smooth, then remove the bowl from the pan; reserve the pan of simmering water. In another bowl, whisk the sugar, flour and salt; mix into the melted chocolate. Add the eggs, one at a time, then whisk in the vanilla until smooth.

2 Divide the batter among the prepared mini-muffin cups, filling each cup three-quarters of the way. Bake until the cakes spring back when touched, 15 to 18 minutes. Let cool slightly. Remove from the pans and let cool completely on a rack.

3 Meanwhile, make the icing: Whisk the sugar, egg whites, lemon juice and salt by hand in the bowl of a stand mixer. Empty the tea bags and add the loose tea to the bowl, then set the bowl over the saucepan of simmering water and whisk until the mixture is hot and the sugar dissolves, about 2 minutes. Transfer the bowl to the stand mixer and beat with the whisk attachment on medium-high speed until the mixture holds stiff peaks, about 5 minutes. Transfer to a large resealable plastic bag, snip a corner and pipe the icing onto the cakes.

MINT PATTY CAKES

MAKES 24 CUPCAKES

ACTIVE: 1 hr
TOTAL: 2 hr

FOR THE CUPCAKES

- 3 sticks unsalted butter, cut into pieces
- 1 cup unsweetened Dutch-process cocoa powder
- 3¼ cups packed dark brown sugar
- 3 cups all-purpose flour
- 1 teaspoon baking powder
- ½ teaspoon baking soda
- ¾ teaspoon salt
- 1¼ cups buttermilk
- 2 large eggs, at room temperature
- 2 teaspoons vanilla extract

FOR THE TOPPING

- 1 pound confectioners' sugar (about 4 cups)
- ½ cup light corn syrup
- ¼ cup vegetable shortening, at room temperature
- 2 teaspoons peppermint extract

FOR THE GLAZE

- 8 ounces bittersweet chocolate, finely chopped
- ¼ cup light corn syrup
- 1½ tablespoons unsalted butter

We modeled these cupcakes after a candy-aisle classic: York Peppermint Patties. Use foil liners for the full effect!

1 Make the cupcakes: Preheat the oven to 350°. Line two 12-cup muffin pans with paper liners. Put the butter, cocoa powder and ¾ cup water in a medium microwave-safe bowl, cover with plastic wrap and microwave until the butter melts, about 2 minutes. Whisk to combine, then whisk in the brown sugar.

2 Whisk the flour, baking powder, baking soda and salt in a large bowl. Whisk in the warm cocoa mixture. In another bowl, whisk the buttermilk, eggs and vanilla; stir into the batter until just combined (don't overmix).

3 Divide the batter among the prepared muffin cups, filling each cup about three-quarters of the way. Bake until the cupcakes spring back when touched, about 30 minutes. Let cool in the pans 10 minutes, then transfer to racks to cool completely.

4 Make the topping: Beat the confectioners' sugar, corn syrup, shortening and peppermint extract with a mixer until a tight paste forms. Gather into a ball, place between 2 sheets of parchment paper and roll out to ¼ inch thick (microwave 15 seconds to soften, if necessary). Use a 2½-inch round cutter or juice glass to cut into 24 disks; reroll the scraps. Place a peppermint disk on each cupcake.

5 Make the glaze: Put the chocolate, corn syrup, butter and ¼ cup water in a microwave-safe bowl, cover with plastic wrap and microwave on 50 percent power until the chocolate melts, about 2 minutes. Whisk to combine, then let cool slightly. Spread the glaze over the peppermint topping, leaving some peppermint exposed. Refrigerate until set, at least 20 minutes. Serve cold.

MINI CARROT CUPCAKES

MAKES 48 MINI CUPCAKES

ACTIVE: 1 hr
TOTAL: 1 hr 50 min

FOR THE TOPPING

- 1 medium carrot
- ¾ cup granulated sugar

FOR THE CUPCAKES

- 1¼ cups all-purpose flour
- ½ cup sliced almonds
- 1 teaspoon baking powder
- ½ teaspoon baking soda
- ½ teaspoon salt
- 1 teaspoon ground cinnamon
- ½ teaspoon ground ginger
- ¼ teaspoon ground allspice
- 1½ cups grated carrots
- ⅔ cup vegetable oil
- 1 cup granulated sugar
- 3 large eggs
- 1 teaspoon vanilla extract

FOR THE FROSTING

- 2½ cups confectioners' sugar
- 8 ounces cream cheese, at room temperature
- 2 tablespoons unsalted butter, at room temperature
- 1 teaspoon fresh lemon juice
- ¼ teaspoon almond extract

The candied carrot topping makes these cupcakes stand out, and all you need is a carrot and some sugar!

1 Make the topping: Peel long ribbons from the carrot using a vegetable peeler, then slice the ribbons lengthwise into ¼-inch-wide strands (you'll need at least 48 strands).

2 Preheat the oven to 250°. Bring the granulated sugar and ¾ cup water to a simmer in a saucepan over medium heat. Add the carrot strands and simmer until soft, about 10 minutes. Drain and let cool slightly. Arrange the strands in squiggles on a parchment-lined baking sheet. Bake until dry, 25 to 30 minutes. Let cool completely.

3 Make the cupcakes: Increase the oven temperature to 350°. Line two 24-cup mini-muffin pans with paper liners. Put the flour, almonds, baking powder, baking soda, salt, cinnamon, ginger and allspice in a food processor and pulse until the nuts are finely ground.

4 Whisk the grated carrots, vegetable oil, granulated sugar, eggs and vanilla in a large bowl until combined. Stir in the flour mixture until just combined. Divide among the mini-muffin cups, filling each cup three-quarters of the way. Bake until a toothpick comes out clean, 10 to 15 minutes. Transfer to racks and let cool 5 minutes, then remove the cupcakes from the pans to cool completely.

5 Meanwhile, make the frosting: Beat the confectioners' sugar, cream cheese and butter with a mixer until fluffy. Beat in the lemon juice and almond extract. Transfer to a pastry bag fitted with a star tip and pipe onto the cupcakes. Top with the candied carrots.

MINI PEANUT BUTTER–CHOCOLATE CUPCAKES

MAKES 24 MINI CUPCAKES

ACTIVE: 1 hr

TOTAL: 1 hr 45 min

FOR THE CUPCAKES

- 1½ sticks (12 tablespoons) unsalted butter, cut into pieces
- ½ cup unsweetened Dutch-process cocoa powder
- 1⅓ cups packed dark brown sugar
- 1⅓ cups all-purpose flour
- ½ teaspoon baking powder
- ¼ teaspoon baking soda
- ½ teaspoon salt
- ⅓ cup buttermilk
- 1 large egg, at room temperature
- 1 teaspoon vanilla extract

FOR THE TOPPING

- ½ cup heavy cream
- 1 10-ounce bag peanut butter chips

FOR THE GLAZE

- 1 tablespoon unsalted butter
- 6 ounces milk chocolate, finely chopped

Use a pastry bag as a batter dispenser when you make mini cupcakes: You won't make a mess!

1 Make the cupcakes: Preheat the oven to 350°, using the convection setting, if available. Line a 24-cup mini-muffin pan with paper liners. Combine the butter, cocoa powder and ¼ cup water in a microwave-safe bowl, cover with plastic wrap and microwave until the butter melts, about 2 minutes. Whisk to combine, then whisk in the brown sugar.

2 Whisk the flour, baking powder, baking soda and salt in a large bowl. Whisk in the warm cocoa mixture. In another bowl, whisk the buttermilk, egg and vanilla; stir into the batter until just combined (don't overmix).

3 Divide the batter among the prepared mini-muffin cups, filling each cup three-quarters of the way. Bake until the cupcakes spring back when touched, about 20 minutes. Let cool in the pan 5 minutes, then transfer to a rack to cool completely.

4 Make the topping: Bring the cream to a simmer in a small saucepan, then pour over the peanut butter chips in a bowl and let stand until the chips melt, about 5 minutes. Whisk until smooth. Refrigerate until the topping is set, about 10 minutes, then beat with a mixer until fluffy. Transfer to a pastry bag with a 1-inch round tip and pipe peaks onto each cupcake. Place in the freezer while you make the glaze.

5 Make the glaze: Put the butter, chocolate and 3 tablespoons hot water in a small, deep microwave-safe bowl, cover with plastic wrap and microwave on 50% power until the chocolate melts, about 2 minutes. Whisk until smooth. Dip the frozen peaks of each cupcake into the glaze, letting the excess drip off. Refrigerate until set, about 5 minutes.

CHERRY-PISTACHIO TEA CAKES

MAKES 12 TEA CAKES

ACTIVE: 15 min
TOTAL: 45 min

- ½ cup pistachios
- ⅓ cup all-purpose flour
- 1 teaspoon baking powder
- ¼ teaspoon salt
- ⅔ cup confectioners' sugar, plus more for dusting
- 2 large eggs
- 6 tablespoons unsalted butter, melted
-   Medium cherries with stems, for topping

We baked whole cherries—stems and all—into these simple tea cakes. Be sure to tell guests that they have pits!

1 Preheat the oven to 350°. Line a 12-cup muffin pan with paper liners. Pulse the pistachios, flour, baking powder and salt in a food processor until finely ground.

2 Whisk the confectioners' sugar and eggs in a large bowl, then whisk in the pistachio mixture until just combined. Stir in the melted butter until just incorporated.

3 Spoon 2 tablespoons batter into each muffin cup. Bake until slightly puffed and just beginning to set, about 8 minutes. Place 1 or 2 cherries in the center of each cake and continue baking until the cakes feel springy and the edges are lightly browned, 10 to 12 more minutes. Transfer to a rack and let cool 10 minutes in the pan, then remove from the pan to cool completely. Dust with confectioners' sugar.

VANILLA CUPCAKES WITH SWISS MERINGUE FROSTING

MAKES 12 CUPCAKES

ACTIVE: 30 min

TOTAL: 1 hr 10 min

FOR THE CUPCAKES

- 1½ cups all-purpose flour
- 1¼ teaspoons baking powder
- ¼ teaspoon salt
- 1 stick unsalted butter, at room temperature
- 1 cup sugar
- 2 large eggs, at room temperature
- 2 teaspoons vanilla extract
- ⅔ cup whole milk, at room temperature

FOR THE FROSTING

- 4 large egg whites
- ¾ cup sugar
- Pinch of salt
- 2 sticks unsalted butter, cut into pieces, at room temperature

These are great all-purpose vanilla cupcakes: Try them with any of the other frosting recipes in this chapter.

1 Make the cupcakes: Preheat the oven to 350°. Line a 12-cup muffin pan with paper liners. Whisk the flour, baking powder and salt in a bowl. Beat the butter and sugar in a stand mixer fitted with the paddle attachment on medium-high speed until fluffy, about 4 minutes. Beat in the eggs, one at a time, until combined. Beat in the vanilla. Reduce the mixer speed to medium low; beat in half of the flour mixture, then all of the milk, then the remaining flour mixture until just combined.

2 Divide the batter among the muffin cups, filling each cup three-quarters of the way. Bake until a toothpick inserted into the center of a cupcake comes out clean, 18 to 20 minutes, rotating the pan halfway through. Transfer the pan to a rack and let cool 5 minutes, then remove the cupcakes to the rack to cool completely.

3 Meanwhile, make the frosting: Whisk the egg whites, sugar and salt in a heatproof bowl set over a saucepan of simmering water until the mixture is warm and the sugar dissolves (do not let the bowl touch the water). Remove the bowl from the pan; let cool slightly.

4 Beat the egg white mixture in a stand mixer fitted with the whisk attachment (or with a hand mixer) on medium-high speed until stiff peaks form, 12 to 15 minutes. Beat in the butter a few pieces at a time, then continue beating until smooth. (Don't worry if the mixture looks separated at first—it will come together as you keep beating.) Spread on the cupcakes.

CHOCOLATE AND OLIVE OIL FIG CAKES

MAKES 6 CAKES

ACTIVE: 25 min

TOTAL: 1 hr 15 min

FOR THE CAKES

- ⅓ cup extra-virgin olive oil, plus more for the pan
- ½ cup all-purpose flour, plus more for dusting
- ¼ cup Dutch-process cocoa powder
- ¼ teaspoon kosher salt
- ⅛ teaspoon baking soda
- ½ cup sugar
- 1 large egg plus 1 egg yolk
- ½ teaspoon vanilla extract
- ½ teaspoon finely grated lemon zest
- 6 fresh figs, halved

FOR THE GLAZE

- 4 ounces bittersweet chocolate, chopped
- 2 teaspoons honey, plus more for drizzling
- 2 teaspoons extra-virgin olive oil

  Large pinch of kosher salt
- ½ teaspoon freshly ground pepper, plus more for topping

These are cupcakes for grown-ups: We topped them with a bittersweet chocolate glaze, honey and freshly ground pepper.

1 Make the cakes: Preheat the oven to 350°. Brush a 6-cup muffin pan with olive oil and dust with flour. Whisk the cocoa powder and ¼ cup hot water in a small bowl; let cool slightly. Combine the flour, salt and baking soda in another bowl.

2 Combine the sugar, egg and egg yolk, vanilla and lemon zest in a stand mixer fitted with the whisk attachment and beat on medium-high speed until pale and thick, about 1 minute. With the mixer running, drizzle in the olive oil. Add the cocoa mixture and beat until combined. Reduce the mixer speed to low, add the flour mixture and beat until just incorporated.

3 Divide the batter evenly among the prepared muffin cups. Bake 10 minutes, then top each cake with a fig half and continue baking until a toothpick inserted into the center comes out with a few crumbs, 8 to 10 more minutes. Let cool in the pan on a rack, 20 minutes. Remove the cakes from the pan and let cool completely on the rack.

4 Make the glaze: Put the chocolate, honey, olive oil, salt and pepper in a microwave-safe bowl and microwave in 30-second intervals, stirring, until smooth.

5 Top the cakes with the glaze. Quarter the remaining 6 fig halves and arrange on top. Drizzle with honey and sprinkle with more pepper.

COCONUT CUPCAKES WITH CHOCOLATE AND ALMONDS

MAKES 24 CUPCAKES

ACTIVE: 1 hr 10 min
TOTAL: 1 hr 40 min

FOR THE CUPCAKES

- 2 large eggs plus 4 egg whites, at room temperature
- 1 cup cream of coconut
- 1 teaspoon coconut extract
- 1 teaspoon vanilla extract
- 2¼ cups cake flour, sifted
- 1 cup granulated sugar
- 2 teaspoons baking powder
- ½ teaspoon salt
- 1½ sticks unsalted butter, cut into pieces, at room temperature

FOR THE TOPPINGS

- 2 cups whole milk
- 1 14-ounce package shredded coconut
- 1 tablespoon confectioners' sugar
- ½ teaspoon vanilla extract
- Pinch of salt
- 6 ounces bittersweet chocolate, finely chopped
- 3 tablespoons corn syrup
- 1 tablespoon unsalted butter
- 48 roasted almonds

Look for canned cream of coconut near the drink mixers at your supermarket. Don't confuse it with coconut milk—cream of coconut is much thicker, richer and sweeter.

1 Make the cupcakes: Preheat the oven to 325°. Line two 12-cup muffin pans with paper liners. Whisk the whole eggs and egg whites in a large bowl. Whisk in the cream of coconut and the coconut and vanilla extracts until smooth.

2 Whisk the flour, granulated sugar, baking powder and salt in a large bowl. Beat in the butter, one piece at a time, with a mixer on low speed until the mixture resembles coarse meal, 3 to 4 minutes. Add half of the egg mixture, increase the speed to medium high and beat until fluffy, about 1 minute. Beat in the remaining egg mixture until combined, scraping down the bowl as needed.

3 Divide the batter among the prepared muffin cups, filling each cup about halfway. Bake until a toothpick inserted into a cupcake comes out clean, 18 to 22 minutes. Let cool in the pans 10 minutes; transfer to racks to cool completely.

4 Make the toppings: Combine the milk, coconut, confectioners' sugar, vanilla and salt in a medium saucepan. Bring to a simmer over medium-high heat and cook until the milk is absorbed and the mixture thickens, stirring occasionally, about 15 minutes. Let cool completely. Put the chocolate, corn syrup, butter and 3 tablespoons hot water in a microwave-safe bowl, cover with plastic wrap and microwave on 50 percent power until the chocolate melts, about 2 minutes. Whisk to combine. Keep warm.

5 Top each cupcake with a heaping tablespoonful of the coconut mixture, pressing gently until compact. Spoon 1 teaspoon of the glaze on top; add 2 almonds. Refrigerate until the glaze sets, about 20 minutes.

MINI BACON CHEESECAKES

MAKES 24 CHEESECAKES

ACTIVE: 45 min

TOTAL: 1 hr 20 min (plus chilling)

FOR THE BACON AND CRUST

4 strips bacon, each cut into 6 pieces

3 tablespoons sugar

12 chocolate wafer cookies

2 tablespoons unsalted butter, melted

Pinch of salt

FOR THE CHEESECAKES

1 8-ounce package cream cheese, at room temperature

⅓ cup sugar

1 teaspoon vanilla extract

1 tablespoon all-purpose flour

1 large egg

Make candied bacon your new go-to dessert topping: It tastes great on cupcakes, ice cream and pudding, too.

1 Make the bacon: Preheat the oven to 350°. Line a 24-cup mini-muffin pan with paper liners. Put the bacon pieces in a large skillet and cook over medium heat, stirring occasionally, until almost completely browned, about 4 minutes. Pour off the drippings and reserve. Sprinkle 1 tablespoon sugar over the bacon and cook, stirring, until the bacon is crisp and glazed, about 3 more minutes. Transfer the candied bacon to a plate; set aside until ready to use.

2 Make the crust: Pulse the cookies, melted butter, the remaining 2 tablespoons sugar, 1 tablespoon bacon drippings, and the salt in a food processor until the cookies are finely ground. Firmly press 1 heaping teaspoon of the crumb mixture into each mini-muffin cup. Bake until the crust is set, about 12 minutes. Let cool in the pan on a rack.

3 Make the cheesecakes: Reduce the oven temperature to 325°. Combine the cream cheese, sugar and vanilla in a stand mixer fitted with the paddle attachment; mix on medium-high speed until light and smooth, 4 to 5 minutes. Add the flour and egg and mix until just incorporated, scraping down the bowl as needed. Fill each mini-muffin cup with about 2 teaspoons batter and bake until set, about 20 minutes. Let the cheesecakes cool in the pan on a rack, then transfer the pan to the refrigerator and chill at least 4 hours. Top each cheesecake with a piece of candied bacon.

CRANBERRY CUPCAKES

MAKES 12 CUPCAKES

ACTIVE: 1 hr
TOTAL: 1 hr 30 min

FOR THE CUPCAKES

- 1½ cups all-purpose flour
- ½ teaspoon baking powder
- ½ teaspoon salt
- ¼ teaspoon baking soda
- ¼ teaspoon nutmeg
- 6 tablespoons unsalted butter, at room temperature
- ¾ cup granulated sugar
- 1 large egg, at room temperature
- 1 teaspoon vanilla extract
- ½ cup sour cream
- ½ cup canned whole-berry cranberry sauce

FOR THE FROSTING

- 2 sticks unsalted butter, at room temperature
- 3 cups confectioners' sugar
- ¼ cup canned whole-berry cranberry sauce
- ½ teaspoon vanilla extract
- Pinch of salt
- Dried cranberries, for topping

These cupcakes are stuffed with cranberry sauce! Use the back of a small spoon to make an indentation in each cupcake while still warm, then fill with the sauce.

1 Make the cupcakes: Preheat the oven to 350° and line a 12-cup muffin pan with paper liners. Whisk the flour, baking powder, salt, baking soda and nutmeg in a medium bowl.

2 Beat the butter and granulated sugar in a large bowl with a mixer on medium speed until creamy, about 2 minutes. Add the egg and vanilla and beat until fluffy, about 3 more minutes. Reduce the speed to low; add the flour mixture and beat until just incorporated, about 1 minute. Add the sour cream and beat until light and fluffy, about 2 more minutes.

3 Divide the batter among the muffin cups. Bake until a toothpick inserted into the center comes out clean, about 22 minutes. Let sit until cool enough to handle, then gently press the back of a small spoon into the center of each cupcake to make an indentation. Fill each indentation with a few teaspoons of cranberry sauce. Remove the cupcakes to a rack to cool completely.

4 Make the frosting: Beat the butter and 1 cup confectioners' sugar in a large bowl with a mixer on medium speed until combined, about 2 minutes. Reduce the mixer speed to medium low; gradually add the remaining 2 cups confectioners' sugar and beat until fluffy, about 2 minutes. Increase the speed to medium high; beat in the cranberry sauce, vanilla and salt until combined. Spread the frosting on the cupcakes and top with dried cranberries.

7 TWISTS ON WHOOPIE PIES

MAKES 8 WHOOPIE PIES

ACTIVE: 40 min

TOTAL: 1 hr 30 min

FOR THE COOKIES

   2 cups all-purpose flour

   ⅓ cup unsweetened cocoa powder (not Dutch process)

   1 teaspoon baking soda

   1 teaspoon salt

   10 tablespoons unsalted butter, at room temperature

   1¼ cups packed light brown sugar

   ½ teaspoon vanilla extract

   1 large egg

   1 cup buttermilk
     Cooking spray

FOR THE FILLING

   1 stick unsalted butter, at room temperature

   2 cups confectioners' sugar

   2 tablespoons milk

   ½ teaspoon vanilla extract
     Assorted toppings, for coating

Whoopie pies are the perfect mix-and-match dessert: You can easily flavor the filling, then put out chocolate chips, sprinkles and other fun toppings and let kids assemble their own.

1 Make the cookies: Whisk the flour, cocoa, baking soda and salt in a bowl. In a separate bowl, beat the butter, brown sugar and vanilla with a mixer on medium-high speed until fluffy; beat in the egg. Reduce the mixer speed to low; beat in the flour in 3 batches, alternating with the buttermilk in 2 batches; beat until just combined.

2 Line 3 baking sheets with parchment paper and lightly coat with cooking spray. Scoop 16 mounds of batter onto the baking sheets, about 2 inches apart (about 2 tablespoons batter per cookie); gently form into rounds with damp fingers and smooth the tops. Refrigerate until firm, about 30 minutes.

3 Preheat the oven to 400°. Bake the cookies until they spring back when pressed, 10 to 12 minutes. Let cool 5 minutes on the baking sheets, then remove to a rack to cool completely.

4 Make the filling: Beat the butter with a mixer on medium speed until fluffy; gradually beat in 1 cup confectioners' sugar. Gradually beat in the milk, then the remaining 1 cup confectioners' sugar; beat until smooth, about 3 minutes. Mix in the vanilla.

5 Sandwich about 2 tablespoons filling between 2 cookies; repeat with the remaining cookies and filling. Roll in toppings.

TRIPLE CHOCOLATE

Dissolve 2 tablespoons cocoa powder in 2 tablespoons hot water; beat into the filling. Roll the edges in mini chocolate chips.

SALTY-SWEET

Beat ¼ cup thick caramel sauce into the filling. Roll the edges in crushed pretzels.

COOKIE CRUNCH

Dissolve 2 tablespoons cocoa powder in 2 tablespoons hot water; beat into the filling. Roll the edges in crushed cookies.

CLASSIC

Keep the filling vanilla-flavored. Roll the edges in rainbow sprinkles.

BERRY-NUT

Mix 2 tablespoons raspberry jam into the filling. Roll the edges in crushed nuts.

SWEET LEMON

Beat 2½ tablespoons lemon curd into the filling. Roll the edges in rainbow sprinkles.

COCONUT-CARAMEL

Beat ¼ cup thick caramel sauce into the filling. Roll the edges in toasted coconut.

BLUEBERRY-LEMON WHOOPIE PIES

MAKES 6 WHOOPIE PIES

ACTIVE: 30 min

TOTAL: 1 hr 35 min

FOR THE COOKIES

- 1½ cups all-purpose flour
- ½ teaspoon baking powder
- ½ teaspoon salt
- ¼ teaspoon baking soda
- 5 tablespoons unsalted butter, at room temperature
- ⅔ cup granulated sugar
- 1 teaspoon vanilla extract
- 1 large egg
- ⅓ cup milk
- ¾ cup blueberries
  Cooking spray

FOR THE FILLING

- 4 ounces cream cheese, at room temperature
- 3 tablespoons unsalted butter, at room temperature
- 1 teaspoon finely grated lemon zest
- 1 tablespoon fresh lemon juice
- ½ teaspoon vanilla extract
  Pinch of salt
- 1½ cups confectioners' sugar

To get the right shape when you're making whoopie pies, smooth the mounds of batter with damp fingers.

1 Position racks in the middle and lower third of the oven and preheat to 375°. Make the cookies: Whisk the flour, baking powder, salt and baking soda in a medium bowl. Beat the butter, granulated sugar and vanilla on medium-high speed in a stand mixer fitted with the paddle attachment until light and fluffy, 5 minutes. Beat in the egg until combined. Reduce the mixer speed to low and beat in the flour mixture in 3 batches, alternating with the milk in 2 batches. Fold in the blueberries with a rubber spatula.

2 Line 2 baking sheets with parchment paper; coat with cooking spray. Scoop 12 mounds of batter onto the baking sheets, about 2 inches apart (about 2 tablespoons batter per cookie). Smooth the tops with a damp finger. Refrigerate until firm, 30 minutes.

3 Bake the cookies until lightly golden, switching the position of the pans halfway through, 10 to 12 minutes. Let the cookies cool 5 minutes on the pans, then transfer to a rack to cool completely.

4 Make the filling: Beat the cream cheese, butter, lemon zest and juice, vanilla and salt with a mixer on medium speed until smooth. Beat in the confectioners' sugar on low speed until combined.

5 Sandwich about 2 tablespoons filling between 2 cookies; repeat with the remaining cookies and filling. Serve immediately or refrigerate, covered, overnight.

RED VELVET WHOOPIE PIES

MAKES 18 WHOOPIE PIES

ACTIVE: 35 min

TOTAL: 1 hr 25 min

FOR THE COOKIES

- 1 ounce semisweet chocolate
- ½ ounce milk chocolate
- 1½ sticks (12 tablespoons) unsalted butter, melted
- ½ cup sour cream
- 2 large eggs
- 1½ teaspoons apple cider vinegar
- ½ teaspoon vanilla extract
- 1 tablespoon red food coloring
- 2¼ cups all-purpose flour
- 1 cup granulated sugar
- ¼ cup unsweetened cocoa powder
- 2 teaspoons baking powder
- ¼ teaspoon baking soda
- ½ teaspoon salt

FOR THE FILLING

- 8 ounces cream cheese, at room temperature
- 3 tablespoons unsalted butter, at room temperature
- 2½ cups confectioners' sugar, sifted
- 1 vanilla bean, halved lengthwise and seeds scraped

Vinegar is a key ingredient in red velvet batters: It's important for the leavening process, plus it helps preserve the color.

1 Preheat the oven to 375°. Line 2 baking sheets with parchment paper. Make the cookies: Chop the semisweet and milk chocolates, place in a microwave-safe bowl and microwave at 50% power until melted, about 2 minutes. Whisk until smooth.

2 Whisk the melted butter, sour cream, eggs, vinegar, vanilla and food coloring in a bowl until combined. In another bowl, whisk the flour, granulated sugar, cocoa powder, baking powder, baking soda and salt.

3 Add the flour mixture to the butter mixture in 4 equal batches, whisking each batch completely before adding the next. Stir in the melted chocolate.

4 Scoop heaping tablespoonfuls of batter onto the prepared baking sheets and smooth the tops with a damp finger. Bake, rotating the sheets halfway through, until the cookies spring back when lightly pressed, 8 to 10 minutes. Let the cookies cool 10 minutes on the baking sheets, then transfer to racks to cool completely.

5 Meanwhile, make the filling: Beat the cream cheese and butter with a mixer until smooth. Beat in the confectioners' sugar and vanilla seeds. Sandwich a heaping tablespoonful of filling between 2 cookies; repeat with the remaining cookies and filling. Refrigerate 30 minutes before serving.

Fun Project!

ALPHABET CUPCAKES

Nothing makes kids happier than a personalized treat—particularly when their initials are spelled out in candy! Steal these ideas for candy letters and you can customize a batch of cupcakes for any party. Spell out Happy Birthday or Congrats, or turn this into a DIY treat: Give kids a few different types of candy and let them create their own edible letters.

Gummy cherry

Sour straw, bent

Licorice wheel, partially rolled

Sour twist pieces

Licorice wheel, trimmed and pulled apart

Sour tape, folded

Chocolate-covered jelly ring

Gummy worm

Gummy ring, snipped

Gummy pink grapefruit wedge, trimmed

Gummy strawberries, trimmed

Square candy blocks

Gummy ring, snipped

Gummy fruit slice

Chocolate-covered pretzel, halved

Wafer cookie, halved,
plus 2 small pieces

Gummy cola bottle, bottom trimmed

Mini candy cane

Chuckles jelly candy, trimmed

Sour tape, folded

Licorice wheel, plus 1 small piece

Gummy worms, trimmed

Banana Runts

Circus peanuts, trimmed

Swedish Fish, trimmed

Candy necklace, string removed

COOKIES & BARS

LEMON–WHITE CHOCOLATE COOKIES

MAKES ABOUT 48 COOKIES

ACTIVE: 40 min

TOTAL: 1 hr 40 min

1¾ cups all-purpose flour

1 cup fine semolina flour

1 teaspoon baking powder

½ teaspoon baking soda

½ teaspoon salt

1½ sticks (12 tablespoons) unsalted butter, at room temperature

1 cup sugar

2 tablespoons extra-virgin olive oil

1 large egg plus 1 egg yolk

3 tablespoons limoncello or other sweet lemon liqueur

½ teaspoon vanilla extract

Finely grated zest and juice of 1 lemon

8 ounces white chocolate, chopped

½ cup pistachios, finely chopped

The secret ingredient in these cookies is limoncello, a sweet lemon liqueur from Italy. Store the leftover limoncello in your freezer; it tastes great drizzled over ice cream.

1 Whisk the all-purpose flour, semolina flour, baking powder, baking soda and salt in a large bowl. In a separate bowl, beat the butter and sugar with a mixer on medium speed until light and fluffy, 2 minutes.

2 Whisk the olive oil, whole egg, egg yolk, limoncello, vanilla and lemon zest and lemon juice in a large liquid measuring cup or bowl. Add to the butter mixture and beat on medium speed until smooth. Reduce the mixer speed to low; add the flour mixture and beat until just combined. Cover the dough with plastic wrap and refrigerate 30 minutes.

3 Preheat the oven to 350°. Line 2 baking sheets with parchment. Roll the dough into 2-inch-long, ½-inch-thick logs; arrange about 2 inches apart on the prepared baking sheets. Bake in batches, rotating the baking sheets halfway through, until golden around the edges, about 18 minutes. Let cool 2 minutes on the baking sheets, then transfer to racks to cool completely.

4 Meanwhile, put the white chocolate in a heatproof bowl and set over a saucepan of barely simmering water (do not let the bowl touch the water); stir until the chocolate melts. Drizzle the cookies with the melted white chocolate and sprinkle with the pistachios. Let set at room temperature, about 15 minutes.

SALTED CARAMEL-PRETZEL THUMBPRINTS

MAKES ABOUT 24 COOKIES

ACTIVE: 35 min

TOTAL: 1 hr 30 min

1½ cups broken thin pretzel sticks

2 sticks unsalted butter, at room temperature

⅔ cup sugar

2 large egg yolks

2 tablespoons honey

2 teaspoons vanilla extract

½ teaspoon fine salt

1¾ cups all-purpose flour

½ cup dulce de leche or thick caramel sauce

Flaky sea salt, for sprinkling

Dulce de leche is like caramel sauce but thicker and richer because it's made with condensed milk (or milk and sugar); regular caramel is made with just sugar.

1 Put ¼ cup pretzels in a resealable plastic bag and crush into coarse crumbs with a rolling pin.

2 Beat the butter and sugar in a large bowl with a mixer on medium-high speed until light and fluffy, 3 to 5 minutes. Whisk the egg yolks, honey, vanilla and fine salt in a medium bowl, then add to the butter mixture and beat until incorporated, scraping down the bowl as needed. Reduce the mixer speed to low; add the flour and pretzel crumbs and beat until just combined.

3 Put the remaining 1¼ cups pretzels in the resealable plastic bag and roughly crush with the rolling pin; spread on a rimmed baking sheet. Drop tablespoonfuls of dough on top and roll into balls, pressing so the pretzels adhere. Refrigerate until firm, about 30 minutes.

4 Position racks in the upper and lower thirds of the oven and preheat to 325°. Line 2 baking sheets with parchment paper. Arrange the cookies about 1½ inches apart on the prepared baking sheets; make a deep indentation in each with your thumb. Bake, switching the pans halfway through, until lightly golden, 15 to 18 minutes. Re-indent with the back of a teaspoon, if necessary. Let cool 3 minutes on the baking sheets, then transfer to racks to cool completely. Fill each indentation with the dulce de leche and sprinkle with sea salt.

CHEWY CHOCOLATE CHIP COOKIES

MAKES ABOUT 30 COOKIES

ACTIVE: 30 min

TOTAL: 1 hr 10 min (plus chilling)

- 2¾ cups all-purpose flour
- 1 teaspoon salt
- 1 teaspoon baking powder
- 1 teaspoon baking soda
- 2½ sticks unsalted butter, at room temperature
- 1¾ cups packed dark brown sugar
- ¼ cup granulated sugar
- 2 large eggs, at room temperature
- 2 teaspoons vanilla extract
- 2 cups semisweet chocolate chips

The secret to these soft cookies is the high proportion of brown sugar. Remove them from the oven before they're fully set in the middle—they'll firm up as they cool.

1 Sift the flour, salt, baking powder and baking soda together into a large bowl.

2 Beat the butter, brown sugar and granulated sugar in a bowl with a mixer on medium-high speed until pale and fluffy, about 4 minutes (use the paddle attachment for a stand mixer). Beat in the eggs, one at a time, then beat in the vanilla. Reduce the mixer speed to low. Add the flour mixture and beat until combined. Stir in the chocolate chips by hand. Press plastic wrap directly onto the surface of the dough and refrigerate at least 1 hour or preferably overnight.

3 Preheat the oven to 375°. Line 2 baking sheets with parchment paper. Drop heaping tablespoonfuls of dough onto the prepared baking sheets, about 2 inches apart. Bake until the cookies are golden around the edges but still soft in the middle, about 12 minutes. Remove the cookies from the oven and let cool 10 minutes on the baking sheets, then transfer to racks to cool completely.

ALMOND CORN PUFF COOKIES

MAKES ABOUT 30 COOKIES

ACTIVE: 30 min

TOTAL: 1 hr

- 1 cup sliced almonds
- 6 tablespoons unsalted butter, at room temperature
- ½ cup almond butter
- ¼ cup honey
- ¼ cup granulated sugar
- ¼ cup packed light brown sugar
- 1 large egg
- ½ teaspoon baking soda
- ½ teaspoon baking powder
- 1 teaspoon ground cinnamon
- 1 teaspoon vanilla extract
- ½ teaspoon almond extract
- 4 cups puffed corn cereal (such as Kix)
- 1 cup chocolate chips (milk, dark or semisweet)

There isn't any flour in these, so you can make them gluten-free by using a gluten-free cereal. Just make sure your chocolate chips and baking powder are gluten-free as well.

1 Preheat the oven to 325°. Spread the almonds on a baking sheet and bake until lightly toasted, about 5 minutes; transfer to a bowl. Wipe the baking sheet clean.

2 Beat the unsalted butter, almond butter, honey, granulated sugar and brown sugar in a bowl with a mixer on medium speed until smooth, about 3 minutes. Beat in the egg. Add the baking soda, baking powder, cinnamon, and vanilla and almond extracts and beat until combined, about 1 minute.

3 Add the cereal, chocolate chips and half of the almonds to the dough and mix with a wooden spoon. Form tablespoonfuls of dough into 2-inch balls and arrange on 2 ungreased baking sheets, about 3 inches apart. (Do not line the baking sheets with parchment paper—the cookies may stick to the paper.) Top each with some of the remaining almonds.

4 Bake until the cookies spread out and turn brown, about 12 minutes, rotating the baking sheets halfway through. Let the cookies cool 5 minutes on the baking sheets, then carefully remove to racks to cool completely. (If you have difficulty removing the cookies from the baking sheets, return them to the oven for 1 to 2 minutes to soften.) The cookies will crisp as they cool.

CHEWY OATMEAL-RAISIN COOKIES

MAKES 12 COOKIES

ACTIVE: 20 min
TOTAL: 50 min (plus chilling)

- 1¼ cups rolled oats
- ¾ cup all-purpose flour
- 1 teaspoon ground cinnamon
- ½ teaspoon baking powder
- ½ teaspoon salt
- 1 stick unsalted butter, at room temperature
- ¾ cup sugar
- 2 tablespoons molasses
- 1 large egg
- 1 teaspoon vanilla extract
- 1 cup raisins

For best results, refrigerate the dough for at least four hours before forming the cookies; this will keep them from spreading too much in the oven.

1 Combine the oats, flour, cinnamon, baking powder and salt in a large bowl. Beat the butter, sugar and molasses in a large bowl with a mixer on medium-high speed until fluffy, about 5 minutes. Beat in the egg and vanilla until smooth, about 2 more minutes. Reduce the mixer speed to low, add the flour mixture and beat until combined. Stir in the raisins by hand. Cover the dough and refrigerate at least 4 hours or overnight.

2 Position racks in the upper and lower thirds of the oven and preheat to 350°. Line 2 baking sheets with parchment paper. Form the dough into 12 balls, about 2 tablespoons each, and arrange 3 inches apart on the prepared baking sheets. Flatten with the back of a fork. Bake until the cookies are golden, 15 to 17 minutes. Let cool 5 minutes on the baking sheets, then transfer to racks to cool completely.

PEANUT BUTTER– BACON COOKIES

MAKES 12 COOKIES

ACTIVE: 30 min

TOTAL: 45 min (plus cooling)

- 1¼ cups all-purpose flour
- ¼ teaspoon baking soda
- ¼ teaspoon baking powder
- ⅛ teaspoon ground cinnamon
- Pinch of chipotle or ancho chile powder
- ¼ teaspoon kosher salt
- 5 strips bacon (⅓ pound)
- 4 tablespoons unsalted butter, at room temperature
- ½ cup creamy peanut butter
- ½ cup granulated sugar
- ½ cup packed light brown sugar
- 1 large egg
- 1 teaspoon vanilla extract
- ½ cup roughly chopped honey-roasted peanuts
- ⅓ cup bittersweet or semisweet chocolate chips

Make these cookies as a gift for a bacon lover and package them in a cast-iron skillet—the perfect tool for frying bacon!

1 Preheat the oven to 350°. Line 2 baking sheets with parchment paper. Combine the flour, baking soda, baking powder, cinnamon, chile powder and salt in a large bowl.

2 Cook the bacon in a large skillet over medium heat until crisp, 4 to 6 minutes per side. Transfer to a paper towel–lined plate; reserve 2 tablespoons of the drippings and set aside to cool. Crumble the bacon, discarding any chewy bits.

3 Beat the butter and reserved bacon drippings in a large bowl with a mixer on medium-high speed until smooth, about 1 minute. Beat in the peanut butter until combined, about 1 minute. Beat in the granulated and light brown sugars until creamy, about 4 minutes, then add the egg and vanilla and beat until light and fluffy, about 2 more minutes.

4 Reduce the mixer speed to low; add the flour mixture in 2 batches until just combined. Stir in the peanuts and all but 2 tablespoons each of the chocolate chips and bacon.

5 Form the dough into 12 balls and arrange 2 inches apart on the prepared baking sheets. Flatten with your fingers (the cookies will not spread in the oven); press the reserved bacon and chocolate chips on top. Bake until golden, 12 to 14 minutes. Let the cookies cool 2 minutes on the baking sheets, then transfer to racks to cool completely. Store in an airtight container for up to 3 days.

NUTTY SANDWICH COOKIES

**MAKES 40 TO 50
SANDWICH COOKIES**

ACTIVE: 40 min

TOTAL: 1 hr

- ¾ cup pistachios, almonds, pecans, peanuts or hazelnuts, plus more for topping (optional)
- ½ cup confectioners' sugar
- ¼ cup granulated sugar
- 1 cup all-purpose flour
- ½ teaspoon ground cinnamon
- ¼ teaspoon salt
- 1 stick unsalted butter, at room temperature

  Coarse, raw or brown sugar, for topping (optional)

  Jam, lemon curd, frosting or chocolate-hazelnut spread, for filling

Experiment with different nuts and fillings in these cookies: This basic recipe leads to dozens of possibilities.

1 Preheat the oven to 325°. Line 2 baking sheets with parchment paper. Pulse the nuts, confectioners' sugar and granulated sugar in a food processor until finely ground. Add the flour, cinnamon and salt and pulse until combined. Add the butter and pulse to form a soft dough.

2 Roll heaping teaspoonfuls of dough into balls and arrange 1½ inches apart on the prepared baking sheets. Lightly flatten the balls with your fingers. Sprinkle with coarse, raw or brown sugar. Press a whole nut into the top of the cookies or sprinkle with chopped nuts.

3 Bake the cookies until lightly golden, about 15 minutes. Let cool 3 minutes on the baking sheets, then transfer to racks to cool completely. Spread your choice of filling on the flat side of a cookie; sandwich with another cookie. Repeat with the remaining cookies.

PEANUT BUTTER–JAM MACAROONS

MAKES 15 MACAROONS

ACTIVE: 35 min

TOTAL: 1 hr 20 min

- ¼ cup unsalted roasted peanuts
- ¼ cup almond flour or finely ground almonds
- 1 cup confectioners' sugar
- 2 large egg whites, at room temperature
- 3 tablespoons granulated sugar
- ½ teaspoon vanilla extract
- ¼ cup raspberry, strawberry or grape jam

Don't confuse these macaroons with coconut macaroons. These are a twist on the French sandwich cookies (also spelled *macarons*) made with almond flour and egg whites.

1 Finely grind the peanuts in a food processor. Add the almond flour and confectioners' sugar and pulse to make a fine powder. Sift twice through a fine-mesh sieve; discard any chunks.

2 Beat the egg whites with a mixer on high speed until foamy. Gradually add the granulated sugar and beat until soft peaks form. Add the vanilla and beat until stiff peaks form. Fold in half of the peanut mixture with a rubber spatula. Repeat with the remaining peanut mixture.

3 Line 2 baking sheets with parchment paper. Transfer the batter to a pastry bag with a ¼-inch round tip. Holding the bag perpendicular to the baking sheet, pipe mounds of batter onto the parchment. Tap the baking sheets against the countertop to help the batter settle. Let sit at room temperature until the tops are slightly crusty, about 15 minutes. Meanwhile, preheat the oven to 375°.

4 Bake the macaroons until slightly crisp, 13 to 15 minutes. Slide the parchment paper with the macaroons onto racks to cool. Carefully remove from the parchment paper and sandwich with the jam.

PISTACHIO MACAROONS

MAKES 15 MACAROONS

ACTIVE: 35 min

TOTAL: 1 hr 35 min

- 1 cup confectioners' sugar
- ½ cup unsalted pistachios, chopped
- ¼ teaspoon ground cardamom
- 2 large egg whites, at room temperature
- Pinch of salt
- 2 tablespoons granulated sugar
- 2 drops green food coloring (optional)
- Edible glitter, for dusting (optional)
- Seedless raspberry preserves, for filling

We gave these cookies some sparkle with a dusting of edible glitter. Look for it at baking supply stores.

1 Preheat the oven to 325° and line 2 baking sheets with parchment paper. Fit a pastry bag with a ½-inch round tip.

2 Combine the confectioners' sugar and pistachios in a food processor and grind until powdery. Sift through a fine-mesh sieve into a bowl and whisk in the cardamom.

3 Beat the egg whites and salt in a large bowl with a mixer on medium speed until frothy. Add the granulated sugar and beat until soft peaks form, 2 to 3 minutes. Add the food coloring and continue beating until stiff peaks form, 1 to 2 more minutes. Fold in one-third of the nut mixture with a rubber spatula, then fold in the rest until just combined. Fold the batter a few more times, until it slowly drips off the spatula (it will still be thick).

4 Transfer the batter to the pastry bag. Pipe about fifteen 1½-inch circles onto each prepared baking sheet. Tap the baking sheets against the countertop to release any air bubbles; let stand at room temperature until the batter is shiny and dry, about 15 minutes.

5 Bake, 1 baking sheet at a time, until the macaroons are slightly crisp and the bottoms release from the parchment, 16 to 20 minutes, rotating the pan halfway through. Let the cookies cool 5 minutes on the baking sheet, then transfer to a rack to cool completely.

6 Dust the macaroons with edible glitter. Sandwich with preserves.

CINNAMON PINWHEELS

MAKES ABOUT 36 COOKIES

ACTIVE: 30 min

TOTAL: 5 hr

- 2 cups all-purpose flour, plus more for dusting
- ½ teaspoon baking powder
- ¼ teaspoon salt
- 1½ sticks (12 tablespoons) unsalted butter, at room temperature
- ⅔ cup granulated sugar
- 1 large egg
- ½ teaspoon vanilla extract
- ¼ teaspoon cinnamon extract (optional)
- 1 teaspoon unsweetened cocoa powder
- ¾ teaspoon red food coloring
- 1 teaspoon ground cinnamon
- 1 tablespoon sanding sugar (clear or red), plus more for coating

You can make these in advance and freeze the dough: Follow the recipe through the end of step 2, then wrap the dough log tightly in plastic wrap and foil; freeze for up to a month.

1 Whisk the flour, baking powder and salt in a medium bowl. Beat the butter and granulated sugar in a large bowl with a mixer on medium-high speed until light and fluffy, 3 to 5 minutes. Beat in the egg and vanilla until incorporated. Reduce the mixer speed to low; add the flour mixture and beat until just combined. Remove half of the dough and wrap in plastic wrap. Add the cinnamon extract, cocoa powder and food coloring to the remaining dough and beat until incorporated; wrap in plastic wrap. Refrigerate both pieces of dough until firm, about 1 hour.

2 Dust the dough with flour and roll out each piece on parchment paper into a 10-by-11-inch rectangle. Flip the red dough on top of the plain dough; remove the top piece of parchment and trim the edges. Sprinkle the ground cinnamon and sanding sugar on top. Starting from a short end, tightly roll up the dough, using the parchment to help; roll the log in sanding sugar to coat. Wrap in plastic wrap and refrigerate until firm, at least 3 hours or overnight.

3 Position racks in the upper and lower thirds of the oven. Preheat to 350°. Line 2 baking sheets with parchment paper. Slice the dough log crosswise ¼ inch thick; arrange the slices 1½ inches apart on the baking sheets. Bake, switching the pans halfway through, until the cookies are slightly puffed and golden on the bottom, 12 to 15 minutes. Let cool 5 minutes on the baking sheets, then transfer to racks to cool.

④ TWISTS ON BROWNIES

MAKES 12 BROWNIES

ACTIVE: 25 min
TOTAL: 1 hr 30 min

Cooking spray
2 cups semisweet chocolate chips
1 stick unsalted butter
¾ cup packed light brown sugar
¾ cup granulated sugar
4 large eggs
1 teaspoon vanilla extract
1 cup all-purpose flour
½ teaspoon salt

Make this your new go-to brownie recipe: You can mix it up in dozens of ways. Try some of these easy options.

1 Preheat the oven to 325°. Coat a 9-by-13-inch baking dish with cooking spray. (For easy removal, line the baking dish with foil, leaving an overhang, and spray the foil.)

2 Combine the chocolate chips and butter in a saucepan; stir over low heat until melted. Remove from the heat and whisk in the brown sugar and granulated sugar; let cool slightly.

3 Whisk in the eggs, one at a time, then whisk in the vanilla. Stir in the flour and salt until just combined. Spread the batter in the prepared baking dish. Bake until a toothpick inserted into the middle comes out almost clean, about 45 minutes. Let cool on a rack, then cut into pieces.

TROPICAL BROWNIES

Fold 1 cup chopped macadamia nuts into the batter. Top the finished brownies with vanilla frosting: Beat 1 stick butter, 2 tablespoons milk, 1 teaspoon vanilla and 1¼ cups confectioners' sugar. Sprinkle with toasted shaved coconut.

TOFFEE BROWNIES

Fold ½ cup toffee bits into the batter. Spread in the pan and top with more toffee bits before baking.

BROWNIE POPS

Cut the brownies into small squares; skewer with lollipop sticks. Combine 1 cup chopped semisweet chocolate with 4 teaspoons vegetable shortening in a microwave-safe bowl; microwave in 30-second intervals until melted, stirring. Dip the brownies in the chocolate; top with chocolate sprinkles. Place on parchment until set.

MINT BROWNIES

Use just 1½ cups chocolate chips in the batter. After adding the flour and salt, fold in 1 cup mint chips. Dust the finished brownies with confectioners' sugar.

STRAWBERRY BLONDIES

MAKES 9 BLONDIES

ACTIVE: 20 min

TOTAL: 1 hr

- 4 tablespoons unsalted butter, plus more for the pan
- 1 cup packed light brown sugar
- 1½ teaspoons vanilla extract
- 1 large egg, lightly beaten
- ¾ cup all-purpose flour
- ½ teaspoon salt
- ¼ teaspoon baking powder
- ¼ cup butterscotch chips
- ¼ cup chopped walnuts
- 3 tablespoons strawberry jam

When making bar cookies, line your baking dish with foil so you can easily remove them: Press the foil into the corners and up the sides of the pan, leaving an overhang on two sides.

1 Preheat the oven to 350°. Line an 8-inch-square baking dish with foil; leave an overhang on 2 sides. Butter the foil.

2 Put 4 tablespoons butter and the brown sugar in a large microwave-safe bowl. Microwave until the butter is melted, about 1 minute. Stir in the vanilla. Let cool slightly, then stir in the egg.

3 Whisk the flour, salt and baking powder in a small bowl. Stir into the butter mixture. Stir in the butterscotch chips and nuts and spread the batter in the pan. Drop dollops of jam on top and swirl with a knife. Bake until set, 20 to 25 minutes. Let cool 15 minutes in the pan, then lift the foil and transfer to a rack to cool completely. Remove the foil and cut into pieces.

CLASSIC LEMON BARS

MAKES 24 BARS

ACTIVE: 30 min

TOTAL: 1 hr 15 min (plus chilling)

FOR THE CRUST

Vegetable oil, for the baking dish

1½ sticks cold unsalted butter, diced

2 cups all-purpose flour

¼ cup packed light brown sugar

¼ cup confectioners' sugar

¼ teaspoon salt

FOR THE FILLING

4 large eggs plus 2 egg yolks

2 cups granulated sugar

⅓ cup all-purpose flour, sifted

1 teaspoon finely grated lemon zest

1 cup fresh lemon juice (from about 8 lemons)

Confectioners' sugar, for topping

Bring your lemons to room temperature and roll them against the countertop before you squeeze—they'll yield more juice.

1 Make the crust: Preheat the oven to 350°. Brush a 9-by-13-inch baking dish with vegetable oil and line with foil, leaving a 2-inch overhang on all sides; oil the foil. Pulse the butter, flour, both sugars and the salt in a food processor until the dough comes together, about 1 minute. Press evenly into the bottom and about ½ inch up the sides of the prepared pan, making sure there are no cracks. Bake until the crust is golden, about 25 minutes.

2 Meanwhile, make the filling: Whisk the whole eggs and yolks, granulated sugar and flour in a bowl until smooth. Whisk in the lemon zest and juice. Remove the crust from the oven and reduce the temperature to 300°. Pour the filling over the warm crust and return to the oven. Bake until the filling is just set, 30 to 35 minutes.

3 Let the bars cool in the pan on a rack, then refrigerate until firm, at least 2 hours. Lift out of the pan using the foil and cut into pieces. Dust with confectioners' sugar before serving.

SALTED PRETZEL–MARSHMALLOW BARS

MAKES 16 BARS

ACTIVE: 30 min

TOTAL: 1 hr (plus chilling)

FOR THE BARS

Cooking spray

1½ cups broken pretzel pieces

1¼ cups all-purpose flour

1½ teaspoons baking powder

1 teaspoon kosher salt

1 stick unsalted butter

1½ cups packed light brown sugar

2 large eggs, lightly beaten

2 teaspoons vanilla extract

FOR THE TOPPING

8 marshmallows, halved crosswise

¼ cup peanut butter chips

1 teaspoon vegetable oil

¼ cup semisweet chocolate chips

We covered these bars with marshmallows, then broiled the top until toasted and gooey. Try this trick on brownies, too!

1 Preheat the oven to 350°. Line a 9-inch-square baking dish with foil, leaving a 2-inch overhang on all sides. Lightly spray the foil with cooking spray.

2 Pulse 1 cup of the pretzel pieces in a food processor until finely ground (you should have about ½ cup crumbs). Transfer to a bowl. Whisk in the flour, baking powder and salt.

3 Melt the butter in a saucepan over medium heat. Remove from the heat and stir in the brown sugar. Let cool slightly, then stir in the eggs and vanilla. Stir in the pretzel crumb mixture in 2 additions.

4 Spread the batter in the prepared pan. Scatter the remaining ½ cup pretzel pieces on top. Bake until golden and a toothpick inserted into the center comes out with just a few crumbs, 25 to 30 minutes. Let cool completely in the pan on a rack, then lift the foil to remove the bars from the pan and transfer to a baking sheet.

5 Preheat the broiler. Press the marshmallow halves, cut-side down, in even rows on top of the bars. Broil, rotating the baking sheet as needed, until the marshmallows are golden brown, 1 to 2 minutes; let cool.

6 Put the peanut butter chips and ½ teaspoon vegetable oil in a microwave-safe bowl and microwave in 30-second intervals, stirring, until melted and smooth. Repeat with the chocolate chips and the remaining ½ teaspoon vegetable oil in another bowl. Drizzle the melted peanut butter and chocolate mixtures over the bars. Let harden at room temperature or refrigerate to set before cutting.

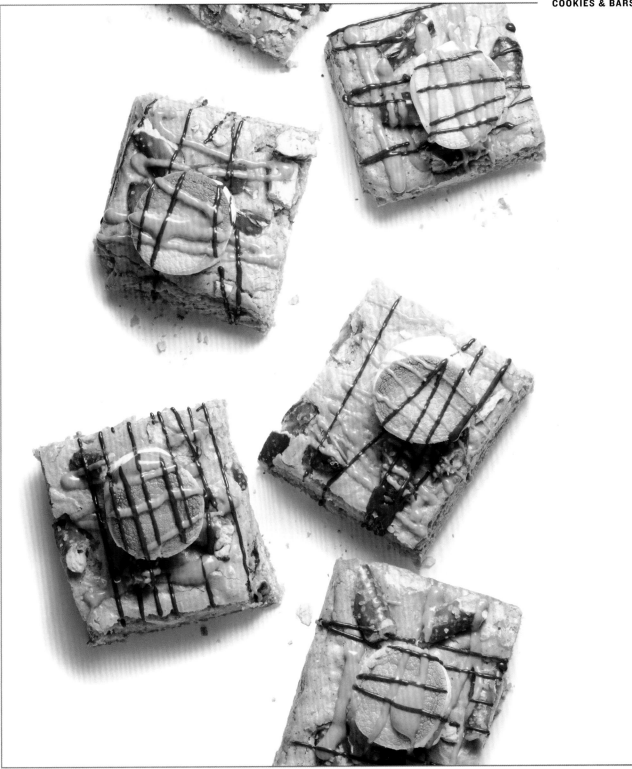

JAM SHORTBREAD

MAKES 9 SQUARES

ACTIVE: 15 min

TOTAL: 1 hr 20 min

1½ cups all-purpose flour

⅓ cup sugar

Pinch of salt

10 tablespoons unsalted butter, at room temperature

6 tablespoons jam or jelly

These bars call for just five ingredients—and you probably have them all on hand! Any flavor of jam or jelly is fine.

1 Preheat the oven to 375°. Line an 8-inch-square baking dish with foil, leaving an overhang. Whisk the flour, sugar and salt in a bowl. Work in the butter with your fingers to make a crumbly dough.

2 Refrigerate 2 tablespoons of the dough for topping. Press the remaining dough into the baking dish; freeze until firm, 10 minutes.

3 Bake the crust for 15 minutes. Spread the preserves on top, leaving a ½-inch border; crumble the reserved dough on top. Return to the oven and bake until the edges are golden brown, 25 more minutes. Let cool 20 minutes, then lift out of the pan and cut into squares.

PB&J CHOCOLATE BARS

MAKES 36 BARS

ACTIVE: 25 min
TOTAL: 55 min

FOR THE CRUMB BASE

- 1 stick unsalted butter
- ⅓ cup granulated sugar
- ⅓ cup unsweetened cocoa powder
- 1 large egg, beaten
- 1 sleeve saltines (40 crackers), finely crushed
- ¾ cup finely chopped roasted peanuts

FOR THE FILLING AND GLAZE

- ¼ cup grape jelly
- 7 tablespoons plus 1 teaspoon unsalted butter, at room temperature
- ⅓ cup creamy peanut butter
- ½ cup confectioners' sugar
- 4 ounces semisweet chocolate, chopped

These bars are inspired by a favorite childhood snack: peanut butter and jelly on saltine crackers.

1 Make the base: Preheat the oven to 350°. Line an 8-inch-square baking dish with foil, leaving an overhang on all sides. Put the butter in a medium heatproof bowl; position the bowl over a saucepan of barely simmering water (do not let the bowl touch the water). Once the butter melts, stir in the sugar and cocoa. Whisk in the egg; cook, whisking, until the mixture is warm and the consistency of hot fudge, 6 minutes. Remove from the heat; mix in the saltine crumbs and peanuts. Press the crumb mixture into the baking dish. Set aside the saucepan of water.

2 Make the filling: Spread the jelly over the crumb base in the baking dish; place the dish in the freezer for a few minutes. Beat 5 tablespoons plus 1 teaspoon butter, the peanut butter and confectioners' sugar with a mixer until light. Spread over the jelly layer; return to the freezer while you make the glaze.

3 Place the chocolate and the remaining 2 tablespoons butter in a heatproof bowl; set over the pan of simmering water and stir until the chocolate is melted. Remove from the heat; stir until smooth. When cool but still runny, spread the glaze over the chilled peanut butter layer. Return to the freezer for another 30 minutes.

4 Bring the bars to room temperature. Use the foil flaps to remove from the pan; cut into squares.

CHOCOLATE CHIP SHORTBREAD

MAKES 18 PIECES

ACTIVE: 30 min

TOTAL: 2 hr 35 min

- 2 sticks unsalted butter, at room temperature
- 1 teaspoon vanilla extract
- ¼ teaspoon salt
- ¾ cup confectioners' sugar
- 2 cups all-purpose flour, plus more for dusting
- 1 cup semisweet chocolate chips

Shortbread can crumble when you slice it. To get clean cuts, score before baking, then score again when the shortbread comes out of the oven and cut along the lines when cool.

1 Preheat the oven to 350°. Line a 9-inch-square baking pan with foil, leaving a 2-inch overhang on 2 sides.

2 Beat the butter, vanilla and salt in a large bowl with a mixer on medium speed until smooth and creamy, about 2 minutes. Reduce the mixer speed to low; add the confectioners' sugar and beat until just incorporated. Add the flour in 2 batches and beat until smooth. Stir in ½ cup chocolate chips with a wooden spoon.

3 Lightly dust your hands with flour and press the dough into the prepared pan. Score the top with a knife to make 9 strips, then score the strips in half to make 18 pieces. Bake until the edges are firm and the top is dry, 40 to 45 minutes. Immediately re-score the cookies, then let cool 20 minutes in the pan. Lift the foil to remove the shortbread from the pan and transfer to a rack to cool completely.

4 Remove the foil. Cut the shortbread into pieces along the scored lines. Put the remaining ½ cup chocolate chips in a microwave-safe bowl; microwave in 30-second intervals, stirring, until melted. Drizzle or pipe over the shortbread and let stand until set, about 1 hour.

Fun Project!
COOKIE PUZZLE

Kids will love this edible puzzle, and you can make it from any basic sugar cookie dough.
Roll out the dough on floured parchment paper until about ¼ inch thick and trim into a rectangle.
Slide onto a baking sheet and bake until golden, about 12 minutes. While the cookie is still warm,
cut into quarters with a paring knife, then cut each quarter into puzzle pieces. Cool completely
before separating. To decorate, mix ½ cup confectioners' sugar with 1 to 2 tablespoons water
until smooth; brush on the cookies and sprinkle with sanding sugar.

CANDY
&
SNACKS

MINI TOASTED STRAWBERRY SHORTCAKES

MAKES 24 SHORTCAKES

ACTIVE: 30 min

TOTAL: 1 hr

- ⅓ cup finely chopped strawberries, plus 24 whole small strawberries
- ¼ teaspoon vanilla extract
- 6 tablespoons sugar
- 1 store-bought angel food cake
- 1 large pasteurized egg white
- ¼ cup marshmallow cream, plus more for topping
- 1 teaspoon fresh lemon juice

  Pinch of salt

Torching a dessert is always a memorable party trick. Pick up a propane blowtorch at a hardware store: It's more effective than the small kitchen torches (and it looks cooler, too).

1 Toss the chopped strawberries, vanilla and 4 tablespoons sugar in a bowl. Set aside until syrupy, about 30 minutes.

2 Trim the tops off the whole strawberries. Cut the angel food cake into ½-inch-thick slices, then use a 1½-inch-round cookie cutter to cut the slices into 24 rounds.

3 Beat the egg white, marshmallow cream, lemon juice, salt and the remaining 2 tablespoons sugar with a mixer on medium speed until stiff peaks form (the mixture may separate before coming together), about 5 minutes.

4 Dip 1 side of each cake round about halfway into the strawberry syrup and transfer to a baking sheet, syrup-side up. Spoon some of the chopped berries in the center. Top with a dollop of marshmallow cream.

5 Swirl the tip of each whole strawberry in the meringue. Then press the strawberry, cut-side down, into the marshmallow cream on top of each cake. Toast the meringue with a kitchen torch or broil until golden, rotating as needed. Serve immediately.

FRUIT JELLIES

MAKES ABOUT 64 PIECES

ACTIVE: 50 min

TOTAL: 50 min (plus chilling)

- 2 **pounds frozen strawberries or peaches, thawed, or 2½ pounds peeled kiwis plus 1 tablespoon lemon juice**
- 3 **cups sugar**
- 5 **tablespoons liquid pectin**

Try a fun twist on these old-fashioned candies: Melt 8 ounces chopped bittersweet chocolate with 2 teaspoons shortening in the microwave; dip the jellies, then refrigerate until set.

1 Puree the fruit; strain through a mesh sieve into a wide saucepan. Stir in 2 cups sugar and boil, stirring occasionally, until a candy thermometer reaches 223°, 30 minutes to 1 hour. Reduce the heat to low and simmer 3 minutes.

2 Meanwhile, line an 8-inch-square baking dish with foil. Remove the fruit mixture from the heat and stir in the pectin. Pour into the prepared pan and refrigerate until firm.

3 Put the remaining 1 cup sugar in a shallow dish. Cut the fruit jellies into squares; toss in the sugar.

CINNAMON RAISIN–NUT TOFFEE

MAKES ABOUT 3 CUPS

ACTIVE: 30 min

TOTAL: 40 min

- 2 cups salted roasted mixed nuts
- 1 teaspoon vanilla extract
- ½ teaspoon ground cinnamon
- ⅛ teaspoon ground cloves
- 1 stick unsalted butter, cut into 1½-inch pieces, plus more for the baking sheet
- 1½ cups sugar
- ½ cup golden raisins

Hands off the spoon! When you're making toffee or caramel, you'll need to stop stirring the sugar once it starts melting: Stirring causes crystallization.

1 Combine the nuts, vanilla, cinnamon and cloves in a bowl. Lightly butter a rimmed baking sheet.

2 Heat the sugar in a saucepan over medium heat, stirring until it just begins to melt. Cook, swirling the pan but not stirring, until most of the sugar has melted, about 10 minutes. Add the butter and cook, swirling the pan, until the mixture is deep amber in color and a candy thermometer registers 300°, about 7 more minutes.

3 Remove from the heat; stir in the nut mixture, then the raisins. Pour onto the prepared baking sheet and spread with a rubber spatula. Let cool completely, then break into pieces.

4
TWISTS
ON
CHOCOLATE BARK

MAKES ABOUT 1 POUND

ACTIVE: 20 min

TOTAL: 1 hr 20 min

- 1 pound bittersweet, semisweet or white chocolate (or a combination)
- 1 cup assorted toppings

The secret to great bark is picking toppings that are different in texture: Choose a mix of chewy and crunchy ones.

1 Line a baking sheet with foil, shiny-side up; smooth out the creases. Chop the chocolate into ½-inch pieces with a large knife. Place all but 1 cup in a microwave-safe bowl. (For swirled bark, put all but ½ cup of each chocolate in 2 separate bowls.)

2 Microwave the chocolate in 30-second intervals, stirring, until melted, 3 to 5 minutes total. (For swirled bark, microwave each chocolate separately at 15-second intervals.)

3 Immediately add the reserved chopped chocolate to the bowl(s); stir vigorously until melted and shiny. Don't worry if there are a few small unmelted pieces.

4 Pour the chocolate onto the prepared baking sheet; use a rubber spatula to spread it into a 10-to-12-inch circle, about ¼-inch thick. (For swirled bark, pour the 2 chocolates side by side on the baking sheet; use the spatula to swirl them together.) Press your toppings into the chocolate. Let the bark harden completely at room temperature, about 1 hour. (If the room is warm, you may need to freeze the bark for a few minutes.) Break into pieces and store in an airtight container at room temperature for 1 to 2 weeks.

BITTERSWEET CHOCOLATE + ALMONDS
+ DRIED FIGS + SEA SALT

BITTERSWEET CHOCOLATE + COCONUT
+ MACADAMIA NUTS + DRIED MANGOES
+ CRYSTALLIZED GINGER

WHITE CHOCOLATE + PISTACHIOS
+ DRIED CRANBERRIES
+ CANDIED ORANGE PEEL

SEMISWEET AND WHITE CHOCOLATE
+ SLIVERED ALMONDS + DRIED APRICOTS
+ FENNEL SEEDS

CHOCOLATE TRUFFLES

MAKES 18 TO 24 PIECES

ACTIVE: 40 min

TOTAL: 40 min (plus chilling)

- 12 ounces good-quality bittersweet or semisweet chocolate, chopped
- 1 cup heavy cream
- 1 tablespoon unsalted butter
- Pinch of salt
- 1 teaspoon vanilla extract
- ¼ cup liquor or liqueur (optional)
- Cocoa powder, chopped nuts, crushed cookies, toffee bits or shredded coconut, for coating

You can make these truffles in advance: Form the chilled ganache into balls in step 3, then cover and freeze for up to 2 weeks. Let them sit at room temperature for 20 minutes before uncovering, then roll in the coatings.

1 Make the ganache: Put the chocolate in a heatproof bowl. Combine the cream, butter and salt in a saucepan over medium heat and bring to a simmer. Pour over the chocolate and let sit until completely melted, about 10 minutes. Stir with a rubber spatula or whisk until smooth. (If necessary, microwave in 20-second intervals until the chocolate melts.) Stir in the vanilla, then add the liquor.

2 Stir the ganache until smooth and shiny, then pour into a shallow baking dish and refrigerate until firm, at least 3 hours or overnight.

3 Line a baking sheet with parchment paper. Roll tablespoonfuls of the ganache into 18 to 24 balls, then roll in your desired coating. Transfer to the prepared baking sheet, cover with plastic wrap and refrigerate until firm, at least 1 hour or overnight.

CHOCOLATE FUDGE

MAKES ABOUT 1½ POUNDS

ACTIVE: 1 hr

TOTAL: 3 hr

- 2 tablespoons unsalted butter, cut into small pieces, at room temperature, plus more for brushing
- 3 ounces unsweetened chocolate, very finely chopped
- 1 teaspoon vanilla, mint or almond extract
- ⅛ teaspoon kosher salt
- 1 cup half-and-half
- 2¼ cups granulated sugar
- 2 tablespoons light corn syrup

  Sprinkles, crushed graham crackers and/or mini marshmallows, for topping

Don't watch the clock—watch your thermometer: Temperature is more important than timing when you're making fudge.

1 Line a 9-by-5-inch loaf pan with foil, leaving a 2-inch overhang on all sides. Lightly brush the foil with butter. Lightly brush the bowl of a stand mixer or another large metal bowl with butter. Add 2 tablespoons cut-up butter, the chocolate, extract and salt; set the bowl aside.

2 Heat the half-and-half in a medium pot over medium-high heat until hot but not boiling. Stir in the granulated sugar and corn syrup and bring to a boil, stirring constantly and scraping the bottom of the pot with a wooden spoon; continue to boil, stirring, until the sugar is dissolved, about 3 minutes. Reduce the heat to low; run a pastry brush dipped in warm water along the sides of the pan to dissolve any sugar crystals clinging to the pot. Clip a candy thermometer to the pot. Simmer the mixture, undisturbed, until the thermometer registers 234° to 238°, 20 to 30 minutes, watching the temperature closely (cooking times may vary). This is the "soft-ball stage." To test for doneness, drop some of the mixture into cold water; you should be able to roll it into a soft ball.

3 Quickly pour the sugar mixture over the chocolate-butter mixture (do not scrape the sides or bottom of the saucepan in case any sugar crystals formed). Clean the candy thermometer, then clip it to the bowl. Let the mixture cool, undisturbed, until it registers 110° to 115°, about 1 hour. (For faster cooling, set the bowl in a larger bowl of cold water.)

4 Brush the paddle attachment or mixer beaters with butter. Beat the mixture on medium speed until just incorporated, about 1 minute. Reduce the mixer speed to low and beat until the fudge just begins to lose its sheen and hold its shape, 5 to 15 minutes. Do not overmix, or the fudge will become hard. Use a buttered rubber spatula to scrape the fudge into the prepared pan and pat into an even layer; smooth the top.

5 Press one or more toppings into the fudge, if desired (about ¾ cup total). Let sit at room temperature for 1 hour, then score the fudge into small squares with a knife and remove the foil. For the best texture, let sit at least 1 more hour before slicing.

6 Wrap leftover fudge in plastic wrap and store in an airtight container for up to 1 week at room temperature or up to 2 weeks in the refrigerator. Bring to room temperature before serving.

SEA SALT CHOCOLATE CARAMELS

MAKES ABOUT 64 PIECES

ACTIVE: 25 min

TOTAL: 25 minutes (plus cooling)

Vegetable oil, for brushing

2 sticks unsalted butter

2 cups sugar

1¼ cups light corn syrup

1 14-ounce can sweetened condensed milk

¼ cup unsweetened cocoa powder

Sea salt, for sprinkling

To give these caramels as a gift, cut parchment into small squares and wrap each candy individually, twisting the ends. Then pack in a box or tin.

1 Line an 8-inch-square pan with foil and brush with vegetable oil. Melt the butter in a saucepan over medium heat; add the sugar, corn syrup, sweetened condensed milk and cocoa powder. Bring to a boil and cook, stirring occasionally, until a candy thermometer registers 248°, about 15 minutes.

2 Pour the caramel mixture into the prepared pan, sprinkle with sea salt and let cool. Cut into 1-inch squares.

HONEYCOMB CANDY

MAKES ABOUT 25 PIECES

ACTIVE: 25 min

TOTAL: 25 min (plus setting)

Vegetable oil, for brushing

1½ cups sugar

¼ cup light corn syrup

1 tablespoon baking soda

8 ounces milk chocolate, finely chopped

3 tablespoons vegetable shortening

This recipe is like a science experiment: Baking soda reacts with the rest of the ingredients and the caramel fills up with air bubbles.

1 Brush a rimmed baking sheet with vegetable oil. Bring the sugar, corn syrup and ¼ cup water to a boil in a large saucepan over medium-high heat; cook, without stirring, until a candy thermometer registers 300°, 10 to 12 minutes.

2 Carefully stir in the baking soda (the mixture will bubble), then quickly pour onto the prepared baking sheet. Do not spread. Let harden, then break into pieces.

3 Combine the chocolate and shortening in a microwave-safe bowl; microwave in 30-second intervals, stirring, until melted and smooth. Dip the candy partway in the chocolate, transfer to parchment paper and let set at room temperature. (Do not refrigerate.)

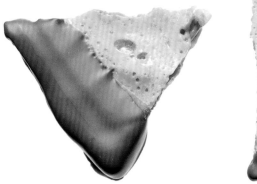

APPLE CIDER DOUGHNUTS

MAKES 12 DOUGHNUTS

ACTIVE: 1 hr 10 min

TOTAL: 3 hr

- 2 red apples, such as Cortland or McIntosh
- 2½ cups apple cider
- 3½ cups all-purpose flour, plus more for dusting
- 4 teaspoons baking powder
- ¼ teaspoon baking soda
- 3½ teaspoons ground cinnamon
- 1 teaspoon salt
- ¼ teaspoon ground nutmeg
- 1⅔ cups granulated sugar
- 3 tablespoons vegetable shortening
- 1 large egg plus 1 egg yolk
- ¼ cup buttermilk
- 1 teaspoon vanilla extract
- ¼ cup confectioners' sugar
- Vegetable oil, for frying

You'll need a 2½- or 3-inch biscuit cutter for these doughnuts, plus a 1-inch cutter for the middles. Don't waste the scraps: Fry them up as doughnut holes!

1 Core and coarsely chop the apples (do not peel). Combine with 1½ cups of the cider in a medium saucepan over medium heat; cover and cook until softened, about 8 minutes. Uncover and continue cooking until the apples are tender and the cider is almost completely reduced, about 5 minutes. Puree with an immersion blender or in a food processor until smooth. Measure the sauce; you should have 1 cup. (Boil to reduce further, if necessary.) Let cool slightly.

2 Whisk the flour, baking powder, baking soda, 1½ teaspoons cinnamon, the salt and nutmeg in a medium bowl. Beat ⅔ cup granulated sugar and the shortening in another bowl with a mixer on medium speed until sandy. Beat in the egg and yolk, then gradually mix in the applesauce, scraping the bowl. Beat in half of the flour mixture, then the buttermilk and vanilla, and then the remaining flour mixture. Mix to make a sticky dough; do not overmix.

3 Scrape the dough onto a lightly floured sheet of parchment and pat into a 7-by-11-inch rectangle, about ½ inch thick. Cover with plastic wrap and refrigerate for at least 2 hours or overnight.

4 Meanwhile, make the glaze: Simmer the remaining 1 cup cider in a small saucepan over medium heat until reduced to ¼ cup. Whisk in the confectioners' sugar until smooth and glossy, then set aside. Mix the remaining 1 cup granulated sugar and 2 teaspoons cinnamon in a shallow bowl; set aside for the topping.

5 Heat 2 inches of vegetable oil in a large heavy-bottomed pot over medium-high heat until a deep-fry thermometer registers 350°. Line a baking sheet with paper towels. Cut the chilled dough into 12 rounds, using a floured 2½- or 3-inch biscuit cutter, then cut out the middles with a 1-inch cutter (or use a doughnut cutter). Slip 2 or 3 doughnuts at a time into the oil and fry until golden brown, 1 to 2 minutes per side, adjusting the heat as needed. Transfer to the paper towels to drain.

6 Dip one side of each doughnut in the cider glaze, letting the excess drip off; dip just the glazed side in the cinnamon sugar. Serve warm.

RAINBOW PETITS FOURS

MAKES ABOUT 50 PIECES

ACTIVE: 30 min

TOTAL: 30 min (plus chilling)

- 1 7-ounce tube almond paste
  Grated zest of 1 orange
- 3 tablespoons orange juice
- 1 teaspoon vanilla extract
- 1 11-ounce pound cake, crumbled
- ½ teaspoon almond extract
  Red, yellow and green food colorings
- 12 ounces semisweet chocolate, finely chopped
- 1 tablespoon vegetable shortening

Traditional rainbow cookies can be tricky to make, but these no-bake treats take just 30 minutes. Look for almond paste in tubes or cans in the baking aisle.

1 Combine the almond paste, orange zest, orange juice and vanilla in a food processor; pulse until combined. Add the pound cake and almond extract; pulse until combined.

2 Divide the mixture into 3 equal portions and tint each with food coloring (1 red, 1 yellow, 1 green), kneading in the food coloring. Pat each color into a 5½-inch square and stack the squares on top of one another.

3 Cut the stack into ¾-inch squares. Set a rack on a baking sheet. Combine the chocolate and shortening in a microwave-safe bowl and microwave in 30-second intervals, stirring, until melted and smooth. Dip the rainbow squares in the chocolate and transfer to the rack; chill until set.

WATERMELON-LIME GELATIN SQUARES

MAKES 16 TWO-INCH CUBES

ACTIVE: 20 min

TOTAL: 4 hr 20 min

8 cups chopped seedless watermelon

¾ cup sugar

2 tablespoons fresh lime juice

1½ tablespoons sambuca or anisette liqueur (optional)

2 tablespoons unflavored gelatin powder (about three ¼-ounce packets)

Cooking spray

About 16 small fresh mint leaves (optional)

We dressed up these watermelon squares for a party with a splash of sambuca and fresh mint leaves; if you're making them for kids, just leave out those ingredients.

1 Puree the watermelon, sugar, lime juice and sambuca in a blender until smooth, working in batches if necessary. Pour through a fine-mesh sieve into a large liquid measuring cup.

2 Pour 1 cup of the watermelon mixture into a small saucepan and bring to a boil. Meanwhile, pour 1 cup of the watermelon mixture into a large bowl and sprinkle the gelatin on top; let stand 1 minute. Pour the hot watermelon mixture into the bowl and stir until the gelatin dissolves. Stir in the remaining watermelon mixture from the measuring cup.

3 Spray an 8-inch-square cake pan with cooking spray, wiping out the excess. Pour in the watermelon mixture. Skim the foam from the surface and refrigerate the gelatin until slightly thickened, about 20 minutes. Arrange the mint leaves on top in rows, then push them just below the surface. Refrigerate until fully set, at least 4 hours.

4 Unmold the gelatin: Invert onto a cutting board, then re-invert onto another cutting board and cut into squares.

GRAPE JELLY BREAKFAST TARTS

MAKES 5 TARTS

ACTIVE: 55 min

TOTAL: 2 hr (plus chilling)

FOR THE TARTS

- 3 cups all-purpose flour, plus more for dusting
- 2 teaspoons granulated sugar
- 1 teaspoon salt
- ¼ cup cold vegetable shortening, cut into small pieces
- 2 sticks cold unsalted butter, cut into small pieces
- ½ cup grape jelly
- 1 large egg, beaten
- ⅓ cup milk

FOR THE GLAZE

- 1 tablespoon granulated sugar
- Juice of 2 oranges
- 2 tablespoons orange liqueur (optional)
- ¾ cup confectioners' sugar
- Grated orange zest, for topping

This butter-shortening dough makes super-flaky tarts, but if you're short on time, just use refrigerated pie dough.

1 Make the tarts: Pulse the flour, granulated sugar and salt in a food processor until combined. Add the shortening and about one-quarter of the butter and pulse until they disappear into the flour, about 30 seconds. Add the remaining butter and pulse a few times, until the mixture looks like coarse meal with pea-size bits of butter. Add ½ cup ice water and pulse once or twice, until the dough just comes together. Turn the dough out onto a piece of plastic wrap, form into a disk and wrap tightly; refrigerate at least 1 hour and up to 1 day.

2 On a lightly floured surface, roll out the dough into a 10-by-14-inch rectangle, about ⅛ inch thick. Cut out ten 4-by-3-inch rectangles using a paring knife or a fluted cutter. Transfer to a parchment-lined baking sheet. Refrigerate at least 15 minutes.

3 Spread 5 of the dough rectangles with a heaping tablespoonful of jelly each, leaving a ½-inch border all around. Brush the edges with the beaten egg, then cover with the remaining 5 dough rectangles. Press firmly to seal, or crimp the edges with a fork. Refrigerate at least 30 minutes. Meanwhile, preheat the oven to 400°.

4 Bake the tarts until flaky and golden, 20 to 25 minutes, brushing with the milk after 10 minutes. Transfer to a rack to cool.

5 Meanwhile, make the glaze: Bring the granulated sugar, orange juice and liqueur to a simmer in a large skillet over low heat; cook until reduced by half, 5 to 7 minutes. Remove from the heat and whisk in the confectioners' sugar until smooth. Let cool. Brush the glaze on the cool tarts, sprinkle with the orange zest and let set, 5 minutes.

CHURROS WITH COCONUT SAUCE

MAKES ABOUT 30 CHURROS

ACTIVE: 30 min
TOTAL: 1 hr

FOR THE SAUCE

- 1 14-ounce can sweetened condensed milk
- ¾ cup unsweetened coconut milk

FOR THE CHURROS

- 1¼ cups whole milk
- 4 tablespoons unsalted butter
- 1 tablespoon sugar, plus more for coating
- ½ teaspoon vanilla extract
- ¼ teaspoon salt
- 1¼ cups all-purpose flour
- 4 large eggs
  Vegetable oil, for frying

Fried food usually needs to be served immediately, but these taste great at room temperature. Fry them up to 2 hours ahead and let sit, uncovered, until ready to serve.

1 Make the sauce: Cook the condensed milk in a medium saucepan over medium heat, stirring constantly, until it turns a light caramel color and starts to pull away from the sides of the pan, 10 to 15 minutes. Gradually add the coconut milk and whisk until smooth, about 5 minutes; set aside. (You can refrigerate the sauce, covered, up to 2 days.)

2 Make the churros: Bring the milk, butter, sugar, vanilla and salt to a boil in a medium saucepan over medium-high heat, stirring, until the butter melts and the sugar dissolves. Reduce the heat to medium low; add the flour and stir vigorously with a wooden spoon until the mixture gathers into a glossy ball, about 1 minute. Transfer to a large bowl and let cool slightly, about 5 minutes. Beat in the eggs, one at a time, with a mixer. Transfer the batter to a piping bag fitted with a ½-inch star tip.

3 Fill a shallow dish with sugar for coating the churros (about ½ cup). Heat about 2 inches vegetable oil in a wide saucepan until a deep-fry thermometer registers 350°. Working in batches of about 6, pipe 3-inch-long segments of batter into the hot oil; use a knife to cut off the segments. Fry, turning once, until golden brown, about 3 minutes per batch. (Return the oil to 350° between batches.) Transfer to a paper towel–lined plate to drain briefly, then roll in the sugar. Serve with the coconut sauce.

GRILLED PINEAPPLE UPSIDE-DOWN CAKES

MAKES 6 CAKES

ACTIVE: 15 min

TOTAL: 30 min

- ½ cup plus 1 tablespoon packed light brown sugar
- 6 tablespoons unsalted butter
- 6 pineapple rings
- 6 maraschino cherries
- 6 shortcake shells

This is one of the easiest desserts imaginable for a cookout. We used shortcake shells (look for them in the produce section near the strawberries), but you can also just slice pound cake into rounds.

1 Preheat a grill to medium high. Lay out 6 sheets of nonstick foil. Mound 1½ tablespoons brown sugar and 1 tablespoon butter on each sheet of foil. Top each mound with a pineapple ring, a maraschino cherry and an upside-down shortcake shell. Bring the foil edges together and fold into a packet, crimping to seal.

2 Grill the packets, sugar-side down, until the pineapple is slightly caramelized, about 12 minutes. Open the packets and carefully flip the cakes so the pineapple is on top.

COCONUT-ALMOND POPCORN BALLS

MAKES 12 BALLS

ACTIVE: 25 min

TOTAL: 25 min

- **2 cups unsweetened shredded coconut**
- **¼ cup light corn syrup**
- **2 tablespoons unsalted butter, plus more for forming**
- **1 cup confectioners' sugar**
- **1 cup mini marshmallows**
- **½ teaspoon almond extract**
- **Pinch of salt**
- **12 cups popcorn**

Butter your hands before you shape the popcorn balls so they won't stick. You'll need to work quickly, though: The mixture hardens as it cools.

1 Preheat the oven to 375°. Spread the coconut on a baking sheet and bake until golden, about 6 minutes.

2 Bring the corn syrup, butter, confectioners' sugar, mini marshmallows and 1 tablespoon water to a boil in a large pot over medium heat, stirring. Add the almond extract and salt.

3 Remove the pot from the heat. Using a rubber spatula, stir in the popcorn until coated. Butter your hands, then shape the popcorn mixture into twelve 3-inch balls and roll in the coconut. Let cool on a parchment-lined baking sheet.

CEREAL BRITTLE

MAKES 15 TO 20 PIECES

ACTIVE: 15 min
TOTAL: 15 min

Vegetable oil, for brushing
1 cup sugar
1 cup cereal (any kind)

Assuming you're sitting on a cereal surplus like most families, try turning it into candy! We used a mix of Cinnamon Toast Crunch, Kix and Cheerios.

1 Line a baking sheet with parchment paper and brush with vegetable oil. Combine the sugar and 2 tablespoons water in a saucepan. Bring to a boil over medium-high heat; cook, swirling the pan but not stirring, until amber, 6 to 7 minutes.

2 Remove the pan from the heat and stir in 1 cup cereal. Immediately pour onto the prepared baking sheet and spread with a rubber spatula. Let cool completely, then break into pieces.

FRUIT LEATHER ROLL-UPS

MAKES 6 TO 8 PIECES

ACTIVE: 45 min

TOTAL: 3 hr 45 min (plus cooling)

> 1¼ **pounds chopped fruit (such as peaches, plums, strawberries, bananas or apples, peeled if necessary)**
>
> ¾ **cup sugar**
>
> 1 to 2 **tablespoons fresh lemon juice**

Fruit leather isn't just for kids! Make a grown-up version by adding 1½ teaspoons grated ginger to the fruit mixture at the end of step 2.

1 Preheat the oven to 200°. Combine the fruit and sugar in a blender. Add the lemon juice to taste (use 2 tablespoons for apples or bananas) and puree until smooth.

2 Transfer the pureed fruit to a medium saucepan and bring to a simmer over medium-high heat. Reduce the heat to medium low and cook, stirring occasionally at first and then more often toward the end, until most of the liquid evaporates and the mixture is very thick, 35 to 45 minutes. Be careful: The mixture may splatter.

3 Line a 12-by-17-inch rimmed baking sheet with a silicone mat or nonstick foil. Use an offset spatula to spread the fruit on the mat or foil into a thin layer. Bake until barely tacky, 3 hours to 3 hours, 30 minutes.

4 Transfer the baking sheet to a rack and let the fruit leather cool completely. Peel off of the mat or foil. If the leather is still moist on the underside, return it to the oven, moist-side up, until dry, about 20 more minutes. Lay the leather, smooth-side down, on a sheet of wax paper and use kitchen shears to cut it into strips on the paper. Roll up the strips and store in resealable plastic bags for up to 1 week.

CONE-OLI

MAKES 6

ACTIVE: 15 min

TOTAL: 45 min (plus chilling)

- 1¼ cups ricotta cheese
- ¼ cup cream cheese, at room temperature
- ⅓ cup confectioners' sugar, plus more for dusting
- 1 teaspoon vanilla extract
- ¼ teaspoon almond extract
- 1 teaspoon finely grated orange zest
- ⅓ cup finely chopped bittersweet or semisweet chocolate (about 2 ounces)
- 6 sugar cones
- 2 tablespoons finely chopped pistachios

These will last for a few hours in the refrigerator, so fill them before dinner, cover and chill, then dust them with confectioners' sugar right before serving.

1 Put the ricotta in a fine-mesh sieve set over a bowl. Refrigerate 30 minutes to drain.

2 Transfer the ricotta to a large bowl. Add the cream cheese, confectioners' sugar, vanilla extract, almond extract and orange zest and beat with a mixer until smooth and fluffy, about 1 minute. Fold in 3 tablespoons chopped chocolate. Cover and refrigerate until thick and cold, at least 1 hour.

3 Transfer the ricotta mixture to a resealable plastic bag. Snip off a corner and pipe the mixture into the cones. Gently press the remaining chocolate and the pistachios into the ricotta mixture. Dust the cones with confectioners' sugar.

Fun Project!
CHOCOLATE-DIPPED TREATS

We can't say that everything tastes better dipped in chocolate, but a lot of things do!
The secret to this snack is tempering the chocolate: Tempering is a process of melting and
cooling chocolate so it is smooth and glossy when it sets. You'll need to pay close attention
to the temperature as you're working. Once the chocolate is tempered, dip your snacks and
place them on a baking sheet lined with parchment and misted with cooking spray.
Let the treats set 30 minutes (set but still soft) to 4 hours (fully hardened).

Popcorn

Soy crisps

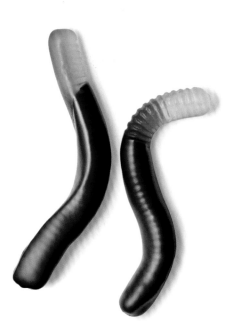

Gummy worms

Large shredded wheat

Dried apples

How to temper chocolate: Finely chop 1 pound semisweet chocolate and combine three-
quarters of the chopped chocolate with 2 teaspoons of vegetable shortening in a microwave-
safe bowl. Microwave in 30 second intervals, stirring, until the chocolate is melted and the
temperature is 100°. Place the bowl in a larger bowl of cold water; stir in the remaining
chocolate until melted (the temperature should drop to about 82°). Remove the bowl from the
water and microwave in 10-second intervals until the temperature reaches 90°.

Grapes

Corn chips

Banana chips

Peanut butter sandwich crackers

Cheerios

Orange segments

Saltines

Doughnut holes

Bacon

Melba toast

Mini toaster waffles

Cheddar cheese

CHOCOLATE-TOFFEE PECAN TART

SERVES 6 TO 8

ACTIVE: 50 min

TOTAL: 4 hr (plus cooling)

FOR THE DOUGH

- 1 cup all-purpose flour, plus more for dusting
- ½ cup unsweetened Dutch-process cocoa powder
- ½ cup confectioners' sugar
- ¼ teaspoon salt
- 1 stick cold unsalted butter, cut into ½-inch pieces
- 1 large egg, beaten

FOR THE FILLING

- 1½ cups pecan halves
- 10 tablespoons unsalted butter
- 6 tablespoons granulated sugar
- 1 teaspoon vanilla extract
- ¼ teaspoon kosher salt
- ⅔ cup light corn syrup
- ¼ cup packed dark brown sugar
- 3 large eggs, beaten
- 3 tablespoons bourbon

You can make the crust and filling a day ahead: Follow the recipe through the end of step 4, then cover and refrigerate the filling and wrap the cooled crust in plastic wrap.

1 Make the dough: Pulse the flour, cocoa, confectioners' sugar and salt in a food processor until combined. Add the butter; pulse until the mixture looks like coarse meal with pea-size bits of butter. Add the egg and pulse once or twice. (Stop before the dough gathers into a ball.) Turn out onto a sheet of plastic wrap and press into a disk. Wrap tightly and refrigerate until firm, at least 1 hour.

2 Place the dough on a large sheet of lightly floured parchment paper. Roll into a 12-inch round, no more than ⅛ inch thick. Invert the dough over a 9-inch tart pan with a removable bottom and peel off the parchment; press the dough into the bottom and up the sides of the pan. (If the dough tears, just pat it back together.) Trim the excess dough. Cover with plastic wrap and refrigerate at least 1 hour.

3 Position racks in the middle and lower third of the oven and preheat to 350°. Line the crust with foil, then fill with pie weights or dried beans. Bake on the middle oven rack, 20 minutes. Remove the foil and weights and continue baking until crisp, 7 to 10 minutes. Transfer to a rack to cool completely.

4 Make the filling: Coarsely chop 1 cup pecans. Combine the butter, granulated sugar, vanilla and kosher salt in a saucepan and bring to a boil over medium-high heat. Cook, stirring, until the mixture turns dark amber, 6 to 8 minutes. Immediately stir in the chopped pecans and cook 1 to 2 more minutes. Remove from the heat and whisk in the corn syrup and brown sugar until dissolved. Let cool until lukewarm, then whisk in the eggs and bourbon until combined.

5 Increase the oven temperature to 375°. Place the tart shell on a baking sheet and pour in the filling up to the brim. Arrange the remaining ½ cup pecan halves on top. Bake on the lower oven rack until the tart is evenly browned and slightly domed in the center, about 40 minutes. Transfer to a rack to cool completely.

PUMPKIN-CHOCOLATE CHIFFON PIE

SERVES: 8 TO 10

ACTIVE: 1 hr 15 min

TOTAL: 4 hr 10 min (plus cooling)

FOR THE CRUST

- 3 tablespoons unsalted butter, melted, plus more for the pie plate
- 24 chocolate wafer cookies (about 5 ounces)
- 3 tablespoons sugar
- ¼ teaspoon finely grated orange zest
- 2 ounces semisweet chocolate, finely chopped
- ¼ cup heavy cream

FOR THE FILLING

- 1 ¼-ounce packet unflavored gelatin
- ¾ cup whole milk
- ⅔ cup plus ¼ cup sugar
- 2 large egg yolks
- 1 15-ounce can pure pumpkin
- 1 teaspoon ground cinnamon
- ½ teaspoon ground ginger
- ¼ teaspoon salt
- 1¾ cups cold heavy cream

You can make this pie a day ahead, but hold off on the chiffon topping until serving time.

1 Make the crust: Preheat the oven to 350° and butter a 9-inch pie plate. Pulse the cookies, sugar and orange zest in a food processor until finely ground. Add the melted butter and pulse to combine. Press the crumb mixture into the bottom and up the sides of the prepared plate. Bake until set, 15 to 20 minutes, then transfer to a rack to cool completely.

2 Combine the chocolate and heavy cream in a small microwave-safe bowl and microwave in 30-second intervals, stirring after each, until smooth. Pour into the cooled crust and spread over the bottom and up the sides; set aside until the chocolate sets, about 20 minutes.

3 Meanwhile, make the filling: Sprinkle the gelatin over 3 tablespoons water in a large bowl; let sit 5 minutes. Combine the milk, ⅔ cup sugar, the egg yolks, pumpkin, cinnamon, ginger and salt in a medium saucepan. Cook over medium-low heat, stirring, until the mixture bubbles, 6 to 8 minutes. Carefully whisk the milk mixture into the gelatin mixture until combined. Let sit at room temperature, stirring frequently, until cool but not set, 30 to 45 minutes.

4 Beat ¾ cup heavy cream in a bowl with a mixer until soft peaks form. Gently fold the whipped cream into the cooled pumpkin mixture, then pour into the prepared crust. Press plastic wrap directly on the surface and refrigerate until firm, at least 3 hours or overnight.

5 Beat the remaining 1 cup heavy cream and ¼ cup sugar until stiff peaks form. Spread on top of the pie.

BANANA-MARSHMALLOW MERINGUE PIE

SERVES 10

ACTIVE: 45 min

TOTAL: 1 hr 15 min (plus chilling)

FOR THE CRUST

- 45 vanilla wafer cookies (about 5½ ounces)
- 2 tablespoons sugar
- Pinch of salt
- 4 tablespoons unsalted butter, melted

FOR THE FILLING

- 25 marshmallows
- ½ cup cream of coconut
- 2 tablespoons unsalted butter
- 1 cup cold heavy cream
- 2 bananas, diced

FOR THE TOPPING

- 2 large pasteurized egg whites
- ½ cup marshmallow cream
- 2 tablespoons sugar
- 2 teaspoons fresh lemon juice
- Pinch of salt
- ¼ cup sweetened shredded coconut

This is not your average meringue pie: The topping tastes like a toasted marshmallow! Before measuring the marshmallow cream, coat your measuring cup with cooking spray.

1 Make the crust: Preheat the oven to 350°. Pulse the wafer cookies, sugar and salt in a food processor until finely ground. Add the melted butter and pulse until combined. Press the crumb mixture into the bottom and up the sides of a 9-inch pie plate. Bake until golden, about 15 minutes. Let cool completely.

2 Make the filling: Put the marshmallows, cream of coconut and butter in a saucepan and cook over medium-low heat, stirring, until smooth. Transfer to a bowl and let cool 15 to 20 minutes.

3 Once the marshmallow mixture has cooled, beat the heavy cream with a mixer on medium speed until stiff peaks form. Fold into the marshmallow mixture. Scatter the bananas evenly over the prepared crust, then top with the marshmallow–heavy cream mixture. Refrigerate until the filling is firm, at least 8 hours.

4 Make the topping: Beat the egg whites, marshmallow cream, sugar, lemon juice and salt with a mixer on medium speed until stiff, glossy peaks form, 5 to 8 minutes. Fold in the shredded coconut and spread over the pie with the back of a spoon. Toast the meringue with a kitchen torch or broil briefly until golden (the meringue will brown quickly).

SUGAR CREAM PIE

SERVES 8 TO 10

ACTIVE: 35 min

TOTAL: 3 hr 10 min (plus cooling)

FOR THE CRUST

- 1¼ cups all-purpose flour, plus more for dusting
- ½ teaspoon salt
- 6 tablespoons cold unsalted butter, cut into ½-inch pieces
- 2 tablespoons cold vegetable shortening

FOR THE FILLING

- 2 cups heavy cream
- 1 cup sugar
- ½ cup all-purpose flour
- ½ teaspoon vanilla extract
- 2 tablespoons unsalted butter, cut into ½-inch pieces
- ⅛ teaspoon ground nutmeg

This classic dessert is often called Hoosier Pie because it's so beloved in Indiana, the Hoosier State: It was declared the official state pie there in 2009.

1 Make the crust: Pulse the flour and salt in a food processor. Add the butter and shortening and pulse until the mixture looks like coarse meal with pea-size bits of butter. Drizzle in 3 tablespoons ice water and pulse until the dough begins to come together (add more water, ½ tablespoon at a time, if necessary). Turn out onto a sheet of plastic wrap and pat into a disk; wrap tightly and refrigerate at least 1 hour and up to 1 day.

2 Roll out the dough into an 11-inch round on a lightly floured surface. Ease into a 9-inch pie plate. Fold the overhanging dough under itself and crimp the edges with your fingers. Pierce the bottom all over with a fork. Refrigerate the crust until firm, about 30 minutes.

3 Place a baking sheet on the middle oven rack and preheat to 425°. Make the filling: Whisk the heavy cream, sugar, flour and vanilla in a bowl. Pour into the chilled crust, dot with the butter and sprinkle the nutmeg on top. Carefully transfer the pie plate to the hot baking sheet and bake 10 minutes. Reduce the oven temperature to 350° and continue baking until the crust is golden and the filling is bubbly in spots, about 55 more minutes (the center will still jiggle slightly); cover the crust edges with foil if they're browning too quickly. Transfer to a rack and let cool completely. Serve chilled or at room temperature.

APPLE-BERRY COBBLER PIE

SERVES 8 TO 10

ACTIVE: 45 min

TOTAL: 3 hr 5 min (plus cooling)

FOR THE CRUST AND FILLING

- 1 piece refrigerated pie dough
- 2 tablespoons all-purpose flour, plus more for dusting
- 3 pounds crisp apples (such as Braeburn or Empire)
- ⅔ cup granulated sugar
- 2 tablespoons fresh lemon juice
- 3 tablespoons unsalted butter
- ½ teaspoon ground cinnamon or apple pie spice
- ¼ teaspoon salt
- 1½ cups mixed berries

FOR THE TOPPING

- 1 cup all-purpose flour
- 3 tablespoons granulated sugar
- 1 teaspoon baking powder
- ⅛ teaspoon baking soda
  Pinch of ground nutmeg
  Pinch of salt
- 4 tablespoons cold unsalted butter, cut into small pieces
- ½ cup buttermilk
  Turbinado sugar, for sprinkling

This is the ultimate hybrid dessert: cobbler meets pie! You can make the filling up to two days ahead; cover and refrigerate.

1 Prepare the crust: Roll out the dough into a 12-inch round on a lightly floured surface. Ease into a 9-inch pie plate, fold the overhanging dough under itself and crimp the edges with your fingers. Chill 30 minutes.

2 Position a rack in the lower third of the oven and preheat to 350°. Line the dough with foil and fill with pie weights or dried beans. Bake until golden around the edges, about 20 minutes. Remove the foil and weights and continue baking until golden all over, 10 to 15 more minutes. Transfer to a rack and let cool completely.

3 Meanwhile, make the filling: Peel and core the apples; cut into ½-inch pieces. Toss with the granulated sugar and lemon juice in a bowl. Melt the butter in a large skillet over medium-high heat. Add the apples and cook, stirring occasionally, until slightly softened, 10 to 12 minutes. Add the flour, cinnamon and salt and stir until the juices thicken, 2 minutes. Remove from the heat and fold in the berries; let cool completely.

4 While the filling cools, make the topping: Whisk the flour, granulated sugar, baking powder, baking soda, nutmeg and salt in a large bowl. Cut in 3 tablespoons butter with your fingers until it is in pea-size pieces. Add the buttermilk; stir with a wooden spoon to make a shaggy dough.

5 Spoon the filling into the crust; dot with the remaining 1 tablespoon butter. Drop large spoonfuls of the topping over the filling and sprinkle generously with turbinado sugar. Place the pie on a rimmed baking sheet. Transfer to the oven and bake until the topping is golden, 50 minutes to 1 hour. (Cover the pie with foil if it is browning too quickly.) Transfer to a rack and let cool until set, about 3 hours.

LEMON-HAZELNUT PIE

SERVES 8 TO 10

ACTIVE: 35 min

TOTAL: 2 hr 45 min (plus cooling)

FOR THE CRUST

- 1 cup plus 2 tablespoons all-purpose flour, plus more for dusting
- ½ teaspoon granulated sugar
- ¼ teaspoon salt
- ⅛ teaspoon baking powder
- 2 tablespoons cold vegetable shortening, cut into pieces
- 5 tablespoons cold unsalted butter, cut into pieces

FOR THE FILLING

- ½ cup granulated sugar
- 1 lemon, thinly sliced
- 6 tablespoons unsalted butter, melted
- 2 large eggs
- ¾ cup packed light brown sugar
- ½ cup light corn syrup
- 1 tablespoon all-purpose flour
- 2 teaspoons vanilla extract
- 1 teaspoon fresh lemon juice
- ¼ teaspoon salt
- 2¼ cups hazelnuts, toasted and chopped

The lemon slices on top of this unique pie are cooked in sugar syrup, which makes them soft and sweet. You can eat the whole lemon slice—peel and all.

1 Make the crust: Pulse the flour, granulated sugar, salt and baking powder in a food processor. Add the shortening and one-third of the butter; pulse until the mixture looks like coarse meal. Add the remaining butter and pulse until it is in pea-size pieces. Add 2 tablespoons ice water and pulse a few more times. If the dough doesn't hold together when squeezed, add more ice water, ½ tablespoon at a time, pulsing. Turn out onto a sheet of plastic wrap and pat into a disk; wrap tightly and refrigerate at least 1 hour.

2 Place a baking sheet on the lowest oven rack and preheat to 425° for 30 minutes. Meanwhile, roll out the dough into a 12-inch round on a lightly floured surface. Ease into a 9-inch pie plate; fold the overhanging dough under itself and crimp. Refrigerate 30 minutes.

3 Meanwhile, make the filling: Bring 1 cup water and the granulated sugar to a boil, add the lemon slices and cook 10 minutes; let cool.

4 Whisk the melted butter, eggs, brown sugar, corn syrup, ¼ cup of the lemon syrup, the flour, vanilla, lemon juice and salt in a bowl. Spread the hazelnuts in the crust and pour in the filling. Arrange the candied lemon slices on top. Place the pie on the hot baking sheet and reduce the oven temperature to 325°. Bake until the crust is golden and the filling is set, 45 to 55 minutes. (Cover the edges with foil if they brown too quickly.) Let cool on a rack.

POPPY SEED TORTE

SERVES 8 TO 10

ACTIVE: 1 hr

TOTAL: 3 hr 35 min (plus chilling)

FOR THE CRUST

- 1¼ cups all-purpose flour, plus more for dusting
- ¼ cup sugar
- 1 teaspoon finely grated lemon zest
- ¼ teaspoon salt
- 1 stick cold unsalted butter, cut into ½-inch pieces
- 1 large egg yolk

  Cooking spray

FOR THE FILLING

- ½ cup sugar
- 4 large egg yolks
- 3 tablespoons cornstarch

  Pinch of salt
- 1½ cups whole milk
- 2 tablespoons unsalted butter
- 1 teaspoon vanilla extract
- ½ cup cold heavy cream
- 1 tablespoon poppy seeds

Lemon–poppy seed is a popular flavor combo in muffins and quick breads, but it makes for a killer pie, too.

1 Make the crust: Pulse the flour, sugar, lemon zest and salt in a food processor. Add the butter and pulse until the mixture looks like coarse meal. Add the egg yolk and 2 tablespoons ice water; pulse until the dough begins to come together. Turn out onto a sheet of plastic wrap and pat into a disk. Wrap tightly and refrigerate until firm, at least 1 hour and up to 1 day.

2 Lightly coat a 9-inch tart pan with a removable bottom with cooking spray. Roll out the dough into a 10-inch round on a lightly floured surface. (If it gets too soft, return to the refrigerator until firm.) Ease the dough into the prepared pan and press into the bottom and up the sides, trimming any excess. Pierce the bottom all over with a fork. Refrigerate until firm, at least 1 hour or overnight.

3 Preheat the oven to 375°. Put the tart pan on a baking sheet. Line the crust with foil, then fill with pie weights or dried beans. Transfer the baking sheet to the oven; bake until the crust edges are golden, about 20 minutes. Remove the foil and weights and continue baking until the crust is golden all over, 15 to 20 more minutes. Transfer to a rack and let cool completely. (The tart shell can be made up to 1 day ahead.)

4 Meanwhile, make the filling: Whisk the sugar, egg yolks, cornstarch and salt in a bowl until combined. Heat the milk in a small saucepan over medium heat (do not boil). Gradually whisk half of the hot milk into the egg mixture, then pour back into the saucepan with the remaining milk and cook, whisking, until thick like pudding, about 4 minutes. Whisk in the butter and vanilla. Pour the filling through a fine-mesh sieve into a large bowl. Let cool to room temperature, stirring frequently, about 30 minutes.

5 Beat the heavy cream with a mixer until soft peaks form. Gently fold the whipped cream and poppy seeds into the cooled filling. Spoon into the prepared crust and smooth the top. Cover loosely with plastic wrap and refrigerate until set, at least 3 hours or overnight.

MISSISSIPPI MUD PIE

SERVES 8 TO 10

ACTIVE: 30 min
TOTAL: 3 hr 10 min

FOR THE CRUST

- 9 chocolate graham crackers (1 sleeve)
- ⅓ cup chopped pecans
- 3 tablespoons unsalted butter, melted

FOR THE FILLING

- 1 stick unsalted butter, cut into pieces
- 2 ounces unsweetened chocolate, chopped
- 2 tablespoons all-purpose flour
   Pinch of salt
- 1¼ cups granulated sugar
- 2 tablespoons light corn syrup
- 2 tablespoons coffee-flavored liqueur
- 1½ teaspoons vanilla extract
- 3 large eggs

FOR THE TOPPING

- 1½ cups cold heavy cream
- 1 tablespoon confectioners' sugar
- ½ teaspoon vanilla extract
- 3 tablespoons finely chopped pecans
   Chocolate sauce, for drizzling (optional)

People say this popular dessert got its name because the center is so thick, like the mud along the Mississippi River.

1 Make the crust: Preheat the oven to 375°. Pulse the graham crackers and pecans in a food processor until finely ground. Add the melted butter and process until moistened. Reserve 2 tablespoons of the chocolate crumb mixture for topping, then press the rest into the bottom and up the sides of a 9-inch pie plate. Bake until set, about 10 minutes; transfer to a rack and let cool.

2 Meanwhile, make the filling: Melt the butter and chocolate in a medium saucepan over medium heat, stirring. Remove from the heat, then stir in the flour and salt until smooth. Stir in the granulated sugar, corn syrup, coffee liqueur and vanilla. Add the eggs, one at a time, stirring until smooth. Pour the filling into the prepared crust and bake until set and cracked on top (like a brownie), about 30 minutes. Transfer to a rack and let cool slightly, about 2 hours (the pie should still be slightly warm).

3 Make the whipped cream: Beat the heavy cream, confectioners' sugar and vanilla with a mixer until soft peaks form. Top the pie with the whipped cream, pecans and reserved chocolate crumb mixture. Drizzle with chocolate sauce.

BOOZY CHERRY-CHOCOLATE PIES

SERVES 6

ACTIVE: 40 min

TOTAL: 2 hr 10 min

- ¾ cup turbinado sugar, plus more for sprinkling
- ½ cup light rum
- 1 tablespoon vanilla extract
- ½ teaspoon grated orange zest
- ¼ teaspoon kosher salt
- 3 pounds Bing cherries, pitted and halved
- 3 tablespoons cornstarch
  Cooking spray
- 6 tablespoons cold unsalted butter, cut into pieces
- 1½ ounces semisweet chocolate, chopped (about ¼ cup)
  All-purpose flour, for dusting
- 1½ 14-ounce packages refrigerated piecrust dough (3 pieces)
  Heavy cream, for brushing
  Vanilla ice cream, for serving

These mini pies don't have a bottom crust, so they're extra easy to assemble, especially if you use refrigerated pie dough.

1 Whisk the sugar, rum, vanilla, orange zest and salt in a large bowl until the sugar dissolves. Add the cherries and cornstarch and toss to combine; set aside until juicy, about 30 minutes.

2 Line a baking sheet with foil and coat with cooking spray. Place six 5-to-6-inch ceramic tart dishes on the prepared pan. Add about ¾ cup cherries to each dish using a slotted spoon; top each with 1 tablespoon butter and 2 teaspoons chopped chocolate. Transfer the remaining cherries and their juices to a saucepan; add ½ cup water and simmer over medium heat, stirring occasionally, until thickened, 5 to 7 minutes. Divide among the dishes; let cool completely.

3 On a floured surface, using the tart dishes as a guide, cut 6 circles from the piecrust about ½ inch bigger than the dishes. Place on another baking sheet; refrigerate until ready to bake.

4 Position a rack in the lower third of the oven and preheat to 375°. Top each dish with a piece of dough, pressing the edges against the dish to seal; pierce several times with a knife. Bake 45 minutes, then brush each pie with heavy cream and sprinkle with sugar. Continue baking until golden, about 15 more minutes. Serve with ice cream.

COUNTRY PEACH PIE

SERVES 8

ACTIVE: 30 min

TOTAL: 3 hr 10 min (plus cooling)

FOR THE CRUST

- 3 cups all-purpose flour, plus more for dusting
- 2 tablespoons sugar
- ¾ teaspoon salt
- 2 sticks cold unsalted butter, cut into small pieces

FOR THE FILLING

- 4 pounds peaches, peeled and cut into wedges
- ¾ cup plus 1 tablespoon sugar
- ¼ cup all-purpose flour
- 1 tablespoon fresh lemon juice
- ¼ teaspoon ground cardamom
- ¼ teaspoon ground cinnamon
- ⅛ teaspoon ground allspice
- 2 tablespoons unsalted butter, cut into small pieces
- 1 large egg

If you're intimidated by lattice crusts, this shortcut is great: Just lay the strips of dough on top of each other!

1 Make the crust: Pulse the flour, sugar and salt in a food processor. Add the butter and pulse until the mixture looks like coarse meal with pea-size bits of butter. Add ½ cup ice water and pulse until the dough just starts to come together. Divide the dough between 2 pieces of plastic wrap and form each into a disk; wrap tightly and refrigerate until firm, at least 1 hour.

2 Make the filling: Toss the peaches in a bowl with ¾ cup sugar, the flour, lemon juice and spices.

3 Lightly dust a large piece of parchment paper with flour. Roll out 1 piece of the dough into a 12-inch round on the parchment. Ease the dough into a 9-inch pie plate. Add the filling, mounding it slightly in the center; dot with the butter and refrigerate. Roll out the second piece of dough into a 12-inch round and cut it into ½-inch-wide strips. Lay half of the strips on the pie in one direction, leaving about 1 inch of space between each strip. Lay the remaining strips on top, crossing them diagonally to make a lattice pattern (no need to weave); trim the edges of the strips, leaving a small overhang. Fold the overhanging dough under itself and crimp the edges of the crust with your fingers.

4 Beat the egg with 1 tablespoon water and brush on the crust edges and lattice top. Sprinkle with the 1 tablespoon sugar and refrigerate until firm, about 30 minutes.

5 Position a rack in the lower third of the oven. Place a baking sheet on the rack and preheat to 425°. Put the pie on the hot baking sheet and bake 20 minutes. Reduce the oven temperature to 375° and continue baking until the pie is golden and the filling is bubbly, 50 minutes to 1 hour. (Cover loosely with foil if the top is browning too quickly.) Transfer to a rack to cool completely before slicing.

4 TWISTS
ON
CHOCOLATE CREAM PIE

SERVES 8 TO 10

ACTIVE: 45 min

TOTAL: 1 hr 15 min (plus chilling)

FOR THE CRUST

- 30 chocolate wafer cookies
- 3 tablespoons sugar
- 6 tablespoons unsalted butter, melted

FOR THE FILLING

- 2 cups whole milk
- ½ cup sugar
- ¼ cup cornstarch
- ½ teaspoon salt
- 4 large egg yolks
- 2 tablespoons brewed coffee, cooled
- ½ teaspoon vanilla extract
- 4 ounces semisweet chocolate, chopped

  Whipped cream and/or shaved chocolate, for topping

1 Make the crust: Grind the cookies and sugar in a food processor. Add the melted butter and pulse until moist. Press into a 9-inch pie plate and bake until firm, 18 to 22 minutes. Let cool before filling.

2 Make the filling: Heat the milk in a large saucepan until hot but not boiling. Whisk the sugar, cornstarch and salt in a large bowl, then whisk in the egg yolks, coffee and vanilla. Whisk half of the hot milk into the egg mixture until smooth, then gradually whisk the egg mixture into the pan with the remaining milk. Cook over medium heat, whisking constantly, until the mixture boils and thickens, 3 to 5 minutes. Remove from the heat and whisk in the chocolate until melted. Transfer to a bowl and let cool slightly, stirring a few times to prevent a skin from forming.

3 Pour the filling into the crust; press plastic wrap directly onto the surface and refrigerate until set, at least 4 hours. Top with whipped cream and/or shaved chocolate.

WHITE CHOCOLATE–RUM PIE
Use only ⅓ cup sugar in the filling; replace the coffee with dark rum and the semisweet chocolate with white chocolate. Top with whipped cream and diced mango.

MILK CHOCOLATE–BANANA PIE
Replace the semisweet chocolate in the filling with milk chocolate. Reduce the sugar to ⅓ cup and add 1 tablespoon cocoa powder with the sugar. Layer 2 sliced bananas in the crust, then add the filling. Top with chocolate sprinkles.

S'MORES PIE
Use 14 graham cracker sheets for the crust instead of the chocolate cookies; bake and let cool, then brush with 4 ounces melted bittersweet chocolate and chill. Make half of the filling; spread in the crust and chill. Beat 3 egg whites, 1 teaspoon cream of tartar and 1¼ cups confectioners' sugar in a heatproof bowl over simmering water with a mixer until the sugar dissolves. Remove from the heat and beat until stiff. Spread on the pie and broil or torch until golden.

CHOCOLATE-RASPBERRY PIE
Replace the coffee in the filling with raspberry liqueur. Top with raspberries and dust with confectioners' sugar.

CHERRY-PEACH GALETTE

SERVES 6

ACTIVE: 25 min

TOTAL: 1 hr 30 min (plus chilling)

- 2 tablespoons unsalted butter
- 2 sheets frozen puff pastry (one 17-to-18-ounce package), thawed
- 3 tablespoons all-purpose flour, plus more for dusting
- 1 large egg
- ½ cup sugar
- ¼ teaspoon ground allspice
- 2 teaspoons vanilla extract
- ½ teaspoon finely grated lemon zest
- 2 teaspoons fresh lemon juice
- 2½ cups cherries (about 1 pound), pitted and halved
- 2 ripe peaches, peeled, pitted and cut into ½-inch-thick wedges

Try turning leftover galette into a milkshake! Blend 1 slice with ⅓ cup milk and about 1 cup of vanilla ice cream.

1 Butter a baking sheet with 1 tablespoon butter. Unfold 1 sheet puff pastry on a floured surface. Beat the egg with 1 tablespoon water and brush over the dough. Unfold the other sheet of puff pastry and lay it on top; press the sheets together with a rolling pin, then roll out into a 14-inch square. Transfer to the prepared baking sheet and refrigerate until firm, about 30 minutes. (Refrigerate the leftover egg wash for brushing the galette.)

2 Position a rack in the lower third of the oven and preheat to 450°. Combine the sugar, allspice, vanilla, lemon zest and lemon juice in a large bowl; transfer 2 tablespoons of the mixture to a small bowl and set aside for sprinkling. Add the cherries, peaches and 3 tablespoons flour to the remaining sugar mixture and toss.

3 Trim the edges of the pastry with a pizza wheel or sharp knife to make a 12-inch round. Spoon the cherry-peach mixture in the center, leaving a 2-inch border. Cut the remaining 1 tablespoon butter into small pieces and scatter on top. Fold in the pastry edges over the filling, pleating as needed.

4 Bake the galette until puffed and golden, about 20 minutes. Reduce the oven temperature to 350°. Remove the galette from the oven, brush the crust with the reserved egg wash and sprinkle with the reserved sugar mixture. Return the galette to the oven and bake until the juices thicken and the pastry is cooked through, 30 to 45 more minutes (depending on the juiciness of the cherries). Transfer to a rack and let cool at least 10 minutes so the filling sets.

APPLE-WALNUT GALETTE

SERVES 6 TO 8

ACTIVE: 55 min

TOTAL: 1 hr 35 min (plus cooling)

FOR THE DOUGH

- 1¼ cups all-purpose flour, plus more for dusting
- 2 teaspoons granulated sugar

  Pinch of salt
- 1 stick cold unsalted butter, cut into ½-inch pieces
- 1 large egg

FOR THE FILLING

- 1 cup walnuts
- ¼ cup plus 1 tablespoon granulated sugar
- 1 large egg
- 3 tablespoons unsalted butter, diced
- ¼ teaspoon vanilla extract

  Pinch of salt
- 3 Golden Delicious or other firm baking apples (about 1¼ pounds)
- ¼ cup apricot preserves

  Confectioners' sugar, for dusting (optional)

Some of the filling in this rustic tart might ooze out during baking. Put a sheet of foil or a rimmed baking sheet on the lowest oven rack to catch any drips.

1 Preheat the oven to 350°. Make the dough: Pulse the flour, granulated sugar and salt in a food processor until combined. Add the butter; pulse until the mixture looks like coarse meal with pea-size bits of butter. Beat the egg with 1 tablespoon ice water in a bowl, then add to the processor and pulse once or twice. (Stop before the dough gathers into a ball.) Turn out onto a sheet of plastic wrap and pat into a disk. Wrap tightly and refrigerate until firm, at least 1 hour. Clean the food processor.

2 Meanwhile, make the filling: Toast the walnuts on a baking sheet on the middle oven rack until golden, 7 to 8 minutes; let cool. Process the nuts, ¼ cup granulated sugar, the egg, 1 tablespoon butter, the vanilla and salt in the food processor to make a creamy paste.

3 Line a flat baking sheet (or an upside-down rimmed one) with parchment paper. Roll the dough into a 12-inch round on a floured surface. Roll the dough up onto the rolling pin, then unroll onto the parchment. Spread the walnut filling over the dough, leaving a 1½-inch border around the edges. Refrigerate while you prepare the apples.

4 Increase the oven temperature to 400°. Peel, core and halve the apples, then cut each half into 8 wedges. Arrange over the filling in a circular pattern, slightly overlapping. Fold the edges of the dough inward, pleating it. Sprinkle the apples with the remaining 1 tablespoon granulated sugar and 2 tablespoons butter.

5 Bake the galette until golden, 40 to 45 minutes. Let cool on a rack. Whisk 1 tablespoon water and the preserves in a bowl. Strain; brush over the apples. Dust with confectioners' sugar.

STRAWBERRIES-AND-CREAM TART

SERVES 6 TO 8

ACTIVE: 45 min

TOTAL: 2 hr 25 min

FOR THE CRUST

2 tablespoons vegetable oil

1 large egg plus 1 egg yolk

2 tablespoons cold whole milk

1 teaspoon apple cider vinegar

1¼ cups all-purpose flour

⅛ teaspoon baking powder

3 tablespoons granulated sugar

½ teaspoon salt

6 tablespoons cold unsalted butter, cut into ¼-inch cubes

FOR THE FILLING

1 teaspoon unflavored gelatin powder

¼ cup granulated sugar

1 vanilla bean, split lengthwise and seeds scraped out

1¼ cups cold light cream

1 quart strawberries, hulled and cut into ½-inch pieces

Confectioners' sugar, for dusting

Vanilla beans can be pricey, but we think they're worth the splurge here. To scrape out the tiny seeds, just split the bean lengthwise and run the tip of a paring knife along the inside.

1 Make the crust: Whisk the vegetable oil, egg yolk, milk and vinegar in a bowl. Pulse the flour, baking powder, granulated sugar and salt in a food processor to combine; add the butter and pulse until the mixture looks like coarse meal. Add the milk mixture and pulse once or twice, just to moisten the flour.

2 Transfer the dough to a 9-inch round tart pan with a removable bottom and pat onto the bottom and up the sides. Cover with plastic wrap and refrigerate until firm, at least 30 minutes. Trim the edges, if necessary.

3 Preheat the oven to 350°. Pierce the dough all over with a fork. Line with foil and fill with pie weights or dried beans. Place the pan on a baking sheet and bake 15 minutes. Remove the foil and weights; continue to bake until golden, 10 to 15 more minutes. Beat the whole egg with 1 teaspoon water, then lightly brush over the crust and bake 5 more minutes. Let cool completely on a rack.

4 Meanwhile, make the filling: Sprinkle the gelatin over 1 tablespoon cold water in a bowl and let soften 5 minutes. Put the granulated sugar and vanilla seeds in a saucepan and rub the seeds into the sugar with your fingers. Add 1 cup cream and whisk over medium heat to dissolve the sugar. When the mixture comes to a boil, remove from the heat and whisk in the gelatin mixture. Transfer to a bowl, then set in a larger bowl of ice water and stir with a rubber spatula until the mixture begins to thicken. Add the remaining ¼ cup cream and stir until thick, about 2 minutes. Pour into the tart shell and refrigerate until set, about 1 hour. Before serving, top with the strawberries and confectioners' sugar.

CHOCOLATE-HAZELNUT TART

SERVES 6 TO 8

ACTIVE: 45 min
TOTAL: 3 hr 35 min

FOR THE CRUST

- ½ cup blanched hazelnuts
- 1 cup all-purpose flour, plus more for dusting
- 2 tablespoons sugar
- ¼ teaspoon salt
- 6 tablespoons cold unsalted butter, cut into small pieces
- 1 large egg, beaten
- ½ teaspoon vanilla extract

FOR THE FILLING

- 2 tablespoons cornstarch
- 2 cups heavy cream
- ¾ cup chocolate-hazelnut spread
- ½ teaspoon vanilla extract
- ⅛ teaspoon salt

Call this tart crust-optional: The chocolate-hazelnut filling tastes great all by itself as a pudding!

1 Make the crust: Toast the hazelnuts in a skillet over medium heat until golden, about 8 minutes. Let cool. Transfer ⅓ cup nuts to a food processor. Add the flour, sugar and salt; pulse until finely ground. Add the butter and pulse until the mixture looks like coarse meal. Drizzle in the egg and vanilla; pulse until the dough starts to come together.

2 Turn the dough out onto a sheet of plastic wrap and pat into a disk. Wrap and refrigerate until firm, at least 1 hour. Coarsely chop the remaining hazelnuts and reserve.

3 Roll out the dough on a lightly floured surface into a 12-inch round. Press into the bottom and up the sides of a 9-inch tart pan with a removable bottom, then trim the excess dough. Prick the bottom all over with a fork. Refrigerate until firm, about 30 minutes.

4 Preheat the oven to 350°. Line the crust with foil, then fill with pie weights or dried beans. Bake until the edges are golden, about 20 minutes. Remove the foil and weights and continue baking until golden brown all over, 15 to 20 minutes. Let cool completely on a rack.

5 Meanwhile, make the filling: Whisk the cornstarch into ¼ cup cream in a bowl. Combine the remaining 1¾ cups cream, the chocolate-hazelnut spread, vanilla and salt in a saucepan. Whisk in the cornstarch mixture and bring to a boil over medium heat, stirring and scraping the sides of the pan with a rubber spatula. Once the mixture starts to boil, stir constantly until thickened, 2 minutes. Pour into the crust and swirl the top. Refrigerate until set, 1 hour. Top with the reserved hazelnuts.

EASY PLUM TART

SERVES 6 TO 8

ACTIVE: 55 min

TOTAL: 55 min

- 1 sheet frozen puff pastry (half of a 17- to 18-ounce package), thawed

  All-purpose flour, for dusting

- ¼ cup almonds, chopped
- ¾ cup sugar, plus more for sprinkling

  Juice of ½ lemon

- 2 pounds large plums, halved and pitted
- 6 tablespoons unsalted butter, diced
- 1 vanilla bean, split lengthwise and seeds scraped out

  Vanilla ice cream, for serving

Plan ahead when you're working with puff pastry: It needs to thaw for about 30 minutes at room temperature (or overnight in the refrigerator) before you unfold it.

1 Preheat the oven to 400°. Lay the pastry on a floured surface and cut in half. Sprinkle 1 piece with the almonds and some sugar; lay the other piece on top. Press together with a rolling pin to make a 6-by-14-inch rectangle. Score a 1-inch border with a knife. Pierce the middle with a fork and make small slits with the knife. Transfer to a baking sheet lined with parchment paper, brush with water and bake until golden, 20 to 25 minutes. Let cool on a rack.

2 Stir ¾ cup sugar, 2 tablespoons water and the lemon juice in a heavy pan. Cover and cook over medium-high heat just until the sugar melts. Uncover and cook, swirling the pan, until amber, about 5 minutes. Remove from the heat; add the plums, 3 tablespoons butter and the vanilla pod and seeds. Cook over low heat, tossing, until the plums are soft and the sauce thickens, about 20 minutes. Add the remaining 3 tablespoons butter and swirl to combine. Remove the vanilla pod.

3 Transfer the crust to a platter. Top with the plums and half of the sauce. Serve with ice cream and the remaining sauce on the side.

PEANUT BUTTER–JELLY TART

SERVES 10 TO 12

ACTIVE: 25 min

TOTAL: 1 hr 30 min

- 1½ sticks (12 tablespoons) unsalted butter, at room temperature, plus more for the pan
- 2¼ cups all-purpose flour
- ½ teaspoon baking powder
- ¼ teaspoon salt
- 1 cup peanut butter
- ½ cup granulated sugar
- ¾ cup confectioners' sugar
- 1 large egg
- 1 teaspoon vanilla extract
- ½ cup jelly or jam

Use whatever jam or jelly you like for this grown-up take on a PB&J. We tried Concord grape jelly and it tasted just like the sandwiches we remember from childhood.

1 Preheat the oven to 350°. Generously butter a 9-inch fluted tart pan with a removable bottom.

2 Whisk the flour, baking powder and salt in a medium bowl. Beat the butter, peanut butter, granulated sugar and confectioners' sugar in a separate bowl with a mixer until smooth. Beat in the egg and vanilla. Add the flour mixture and stir with a wooden spoon until combined.

3 Press half the dough into the bottom and up the sides of the prepared tart pan. Spread the jelly over the dough, leaving a ½-inch border around the edges. Drop about half of the remaining dough over the jelly by the tablespoonful; lightly press the rest of the dough into the pan around the edges to form a crust. Bake until golden, 45 to 50 minutes.

4 Transfer the pan to a rack and let cool. Remove the ring and transfer the tart to a plate.

BLUEBERRY-ALMOND CRUMBLE

SERVES 8

ACTIVE: 15 min

TOTAL: 1 hr 5 min

FOR THE TOPPING

- 7 tablespoons unsalted butter, at room temperature, plus more for the baking dish
- ½ cup cornmeal
- ¾ cup all-purpose flour
- ½ cup packed light brown sugar
  Pinch of salt
- ¾ cup chopped almonds

FOR THE FILLING

- 4 cups blueberries
- ⅓ cup granulated sugar
- 1 tablespoon all-purpose flour
- 1 teaspoon fresh lemon juice
- 2 tablespoons cold unsalted butter, cut into small pieces
  Vanilla ice cream, for serving

Use this recipe as a guide and design your own crumble topping: Try oats instead of cornmeal and pecans or hazelnuts instead of almonds.

1 Preheat the oven to 375°. Butter a 2-quart shallow baking dish. Make the topping: Whisk the cornmeal, flour, brown sugar and salt in a bowl. Stir in the almonds. Work in the butter with your fingers until incorporated.

2 Make the filling: Toss the blueberries, granulated sugar, flour and lemon juice in a bowl.

3 Transfer the filling to the prepared dish and dot with the cold butter. Squeeze handfuls of the crumble mixture and scatter on top of the fruit. Bake until golden and bubbly, 40 to 45 minutes. Let sit 10 minutes before serving. Top with ice cream.

NECTARINE-PLUM-BLACKBERRY CRUMBLES

SERVES 8

ACTIVE: 15 min

TOTAL: 1 hr 5 min

FOR THE TOPPING

7 tablespoons unsalted butter, at room temperature, plus more for the ramekins

½ cup cornmeal

¾ cup all-purpose flour

½ cup packed light brown sugar

Pinch of salt

¾ cup chopped pistachios

FOR THE FILLING

4 nectarines

2 plums

2 cups blackberries

½ cup granulated sugar

1 tablespoon all-purpose flour

2 tablespoons cold unsalted butter, cut into small pieces

These individual crumbles are fun, but you can make a full-size one in a shallow 2-quart baking dish. The baking time is the same.

1 Preheat the oven to 375°. Butter eight 6-ounce ramekins. Make the topping: Whisk the cornmeal, flour, brown sugar and salt in a bowl. Stir in the pistachios. Work in the butter with your fingers until incorporated.

2 Make the filling: Halve and pit the nectarines and plums (no need to peel). Slice ½ inch thick. Toss with the blackberries, granulated sugar and flour in a bowl.

3 Transfer the filling to the prepared ramekins and dot with the cold butter. Squeeze handfuls of the crumble mixture and scatter on top of the fruit. Bake until golden and bubbly, 40 to 45 minutes. Let sit 10 minutes before serving.

PEACH-RASPBERRY SKILLET COBBLER

SERVES 8

ACTIVE: 30 min

TOTAL: 1 hr

FOR THE TOPPING

- 1¾ cups all-purpose flour, plus more for dusting
- ¼ cup sugar, plus more for sprinkling
- 2 teaspoons baking powder
- ½ teaspoon salt
- ⅛ teaspoon ground nutmeg
- 1 stick cold unsalted butter, cut into ½-inch pieces
- ⅔ cup heavy cream, plus more for brushing

FOR THE FILLING

- 2 tablespoons unsalted butter
- 5 large peaches, peeled and cut into ½-inch-thick wedges
- 2 tablespoons all-purpose flour
- ½ cup honey
- 1 tablespoon fresh lemon juice
- 1 teaspoon lemon zest
- ½ teaspoon vanilla extract
- ½ teaspoon ground cinnamon
- ¼ teaspoon ground nutmeg
- 1 cup raspberries

To dress up this skillet cobbler, cut the biscuits into shapes with a cookie cutter. Just make sure the cutter isn't too intricate; the shapes lose definition when the biscuits puff up.

1 Preheat the oven to 425°. Make the topping: Whisk the flour, sugar, baking powder, salt and nutmeg in a large bowl. Work in the butter with your fingers or a pastry blender until the mixture looks like coarse meal with some pea-size lumps. Add the cream and stir with a fork until combined. Turn out onto a lightly floured surface; knead 4 or 5 times to bring the dough together. Pat into a ½-inch-thick round, then use a 1½-to-2-inch cookie cutter to cut out biscuits. Pat the scraps together and cut out more biscuits. Put the biscuits on a baking sheet and refrigerate until ready to use.

2 Make the filling: Melt the butter in a large ovenproof skillet over medium heat. Add the peaches, flour, honey, lemon juice, lemon zest, vanilla, cinnamon and nutmeg and cook, stirring occasionally, until bubbling, 5 minutes. Stir in the raspberries, then arrange the biscuits on top. Brush the biscuits with cream and sprinkle lightly with sugar.

3 Transfer the skillet to the oven and bake until the biscuits are cooked through, about 25 minutes. (If the biscuits are browning too quickly, cover loosely with foil.) Let cool slightly before serving.

APPLE-BERRY PIE POPS

MAKES ABOUT 24 POPS

ACTIVE: 45 min

TOTAL: 1 hr 10 min (plus cooling)

- 3 apples (such as Golden Delicious and/or McIntosh), peeled, cored and cut into ¼-inch pieces
- ½ cup raspberries
- 3 tablespoons granulated sugar
- 1 tablespoon fresh lemon juice
- 1 tablespoon unsalted butter
- 2 teaspoons all-purpose flour, plus more for dusting
- ¼ teaspoon ground cinnamon
- Pinch of ground nutmeg
- 2 14-ounce packages refrigerated pie dough
- 1 large egg, beaten
- Turbinado sugar, for sprinkling

These pies-on-a-stick are perfect for a bake sale. Show them off by standing them up in a wide jar.

1 Toss the apples, raspberries, granulated sugar and lemon juice in a large bowl. Melt the butter in a medium skillet over medium heat. Add the fruit mixture and cook, stirring occasionally, until the apples are soft and the raspberries break down, 8 to 10 minutes. Sprinkle in the flour, cinnamon and nutmeg and stir until the juices begin to thicken, about 1 minute; set aside to cool completely.

2 Preheat the oven to 375° and line 2 baking sheets with parchment paper. Unroll the pie dough on a lightly floured surface. Cut out 2½-inch rounds with a cookie cutter or glass (you should get about 48 rounds). Arrange half of the rounds on the prepared baking sheets; put a rounded teaspoonful of filling in the center of each. Brush the edges of the dough with water, then top with the remaining dough rounds, crimping the edges with a fork to seal.

3 Brush the pies with the beaten egg and sprinkle with turbinado sugar. Cut a small X in the center of each to allow steam to escape. Bake until golden, 22 to 24 minutes. Let cool slightly on the baking sheets, then insert a lollipop stick into each. Let cool completely. Store in an airtight container up to 3 days.

Fun Project!
PIE FRIES

Turn your pie-dough scraps into dessert fries! Just roll out the scraps and cut into strips
using a fluted pastry wheel, then arrange on a parchment-lined baking sheet. Brush with
melted butter, sprinkle with cinnamon sugar and bake at 375° until golden, about 15 minutes.
Serve with berry jam for dipping.

FAKE-OUT CAKES

PENCIL CAKE

SERVES 10 TO 12

ACTIVE: 45 min

TOTAL: 1 hr 20 min

- 2 16-ounce frozen pound cakes, thawed slightly
- 1 16-ounce tub vanilla frosting
- 6 drops red food coloring
- 23 drops yellow food coloring
- 2 tablespoons semisweet chocolate chips
- 2 green sour belt candies

Use frozen pound cake to make this edible pencil: It's denser and easier to slice than the kind from the bakery section.

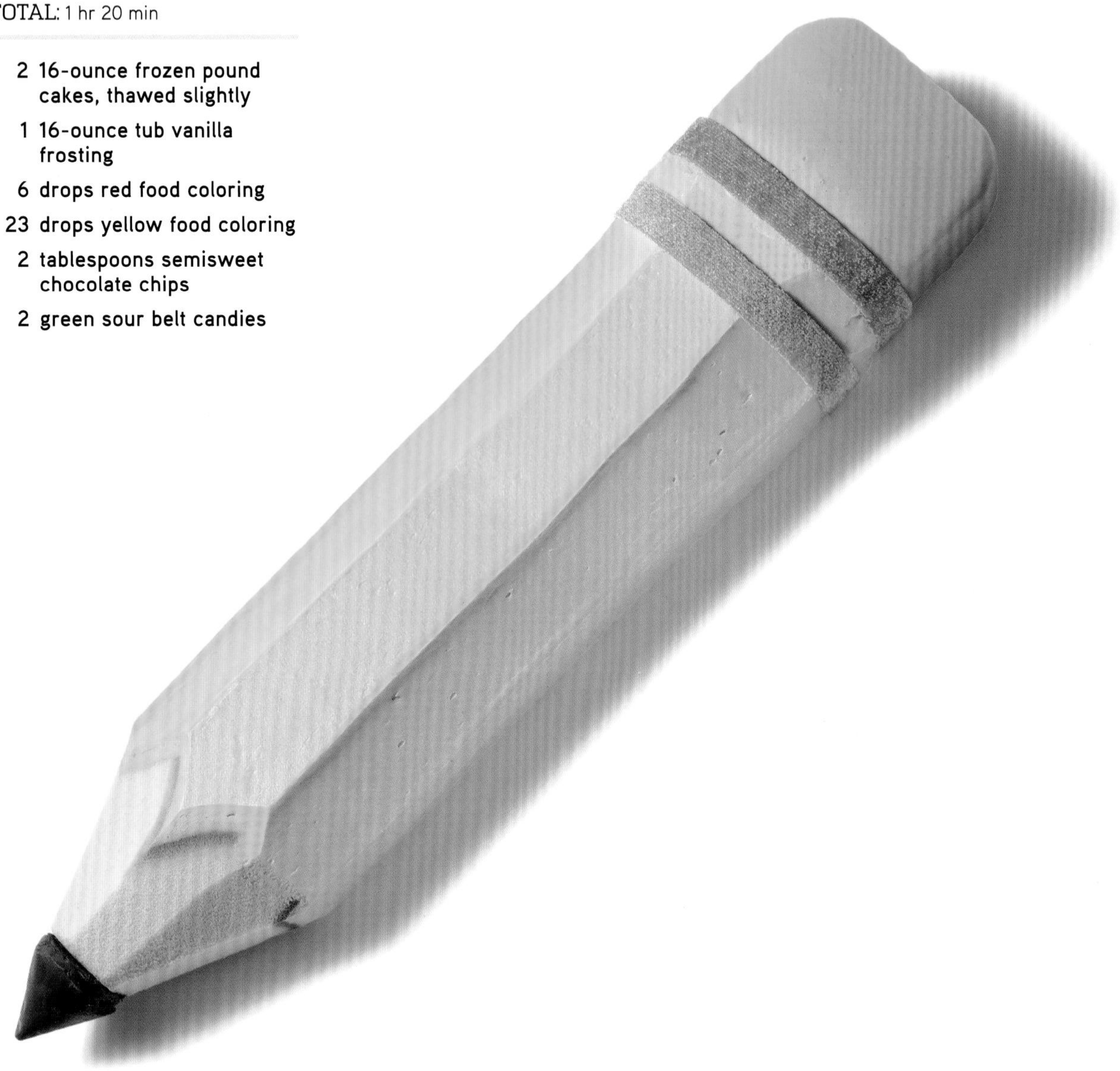

1 Cut a 2-inch piece from one pound cake for the eraser; set aside. Trim ½ inch from the uncut ends of both cakes. Line up the cakes to make one long cake.

2 Using a paring knife, score 2 lines down the length of both cakes, 1¼ inches in from each side. With the lines as a guide, trim the cake sides at an angle as shown.

3 Mix ½ cup vanilla frosting, the red food coloring and 3 drops yellow food coloring in a glass liquid measuring cup. Microwave the frosting about 20 seconds, stirring every 5 seconds.

4 Make the eraser: Put the 2-inch piece of cake on a rack set over a baking sheet. Pour the warm pink frosting evenly over the cake, then refrigerate until set, about 20 minutes.

5 Microwave the chocolate chips in a resealable plastic bag (unsealed) in 5-second intervals until melted. Push the chocolate to one corner, twist the bag and secure with tape; freeze until set.

6 Mix the remaining 1½ cups frosting and 20 drops yellow food coloring. Frost the cake with an offset spatula, following the beveled edges.

7 Make the tip: Cut one end of the cake into a tip, shaving it with a paring knife so the pencil looks sharpened.

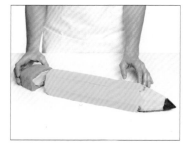

8 Remove the chocolate cone from the bag and trim the base to make it flat. Attach the chocolate tip to the pencil with frosting; attach the eraser to the other end.

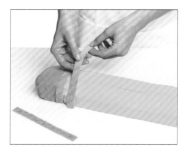

9 Lay the sour belts across the end of the pencil near the eraser, trimming as needed. Gently press into the frosting to secure.

CARAMEL APPLE CAKE

SERVES 14 TO 16

ACTIVE: 50 min
TOTAL: 2 hr

Cooking spray

2 16-to-18-ounce boxes spice cake mix (plus required ingredients)

2 16-ounce tubs vanilla frosting

20 drops red food coloring

2 dashes vanilla extract

10 drops yellow food coloring

70 soft caramels (about 20 ounces)

1 cup cocktail peanuts, roughly chopped

This giant apple cake is coated in caramel just like the real thing. If you unwrap and microwave soft caramels for a few seconds, you can easily roll them into a sheet!

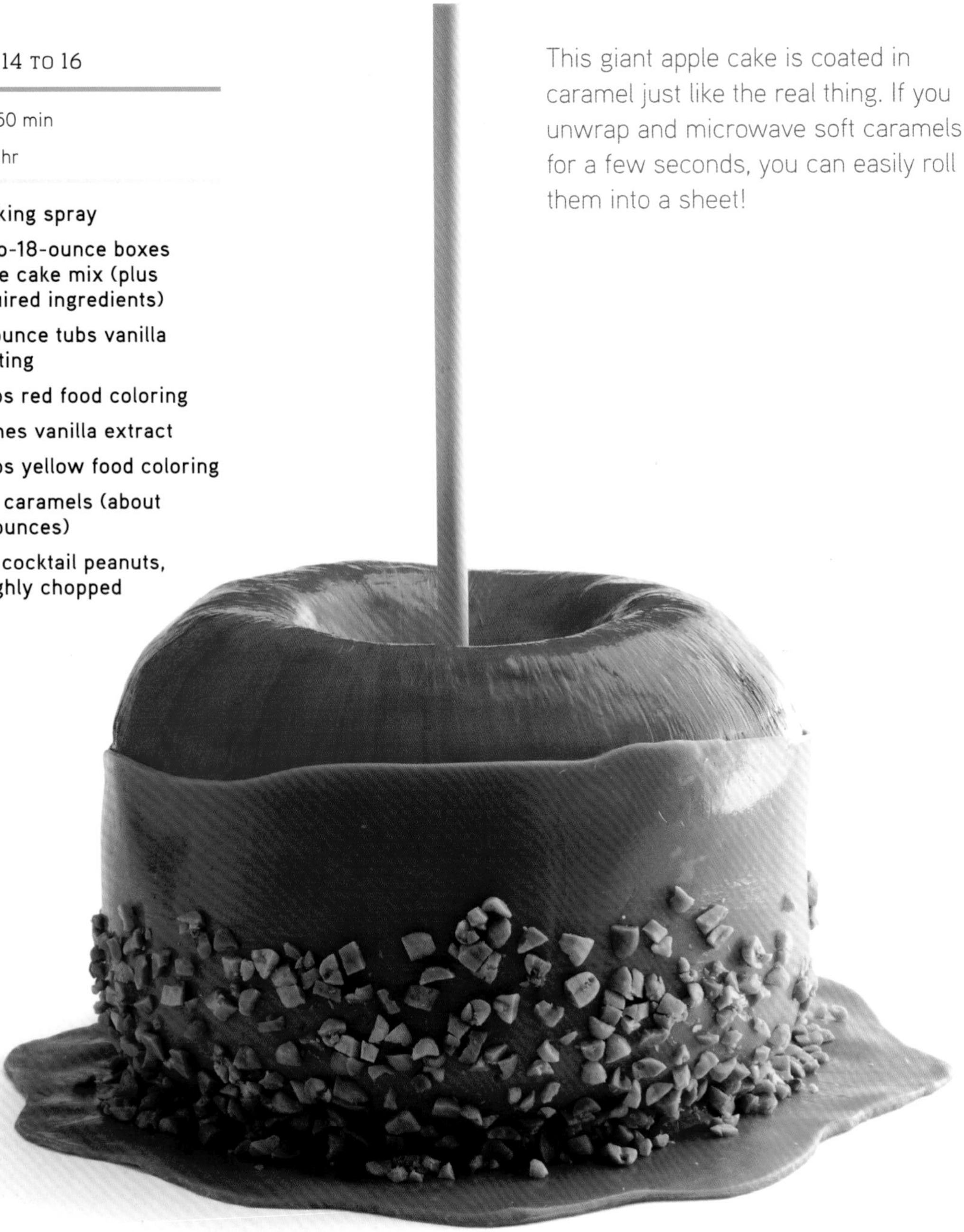

1 Coat four 9-inch-round cake pans with cooking spray (or use 2 pans, in batches). Prepare the cake mixes as directed; divide among the pans and bake as directed. Let cool 20 minutes; remove from the pans.

2 Stack the cakes on an upside-down cake pan, spreading frosting between each layer. Freeze about 30 minutes. Trim the bottom 2 layers of the cake on an angle to resemble the bottom of an apple.

3 Trim the edges of the top cake layer just enough to round them, then carve out a 3-inch-wide cone-shaped piece of cake where the stem would be.

4 Crumble the cake trimmings in a bowl and mix with just enough frosting to moisten. Clump the cake mixture together and mound in a ring around the hole to form the top of the apple.

5 Cover the cake with a very thin layer of frosting (this is the crumb coat). Freeze 20 minutes, then cover the top 4 inches of the cake, including inside the stem cavity, with more frosting.

6 Mix the red food coloring with a dash of vanilla; brush onto the top part of the cake, blotting the brush on a paper towel. Repeat with the yellow food coloring and another dash of vanilla to add yellow streaks.

7 Unwrap the caramels and microwave until soft but not melted, about 20 seconds. Flatten the caramel into a rectangle, then roll out and stretch on parchment into a 7-by-26-inch rectangle.

8 Moisten the caramel rectangle with water where you want the peanuts to go. Sprinkle the nuts on top, then press them in using a rolling pin.

9 Wrap the caramel around the cake, leaving the red frosting exposed at the top. Tuck the caramel underneath the cake, then trim it so it looks like a pool of caramel. Insert a wooden dowel into the cake.

STRAWBERRY PIE CAKE

SERVES 8 TO 10

ACTIVE: 45 min

TOTAL: 1 hr 20 min

Cooking spray

1 16-to-18-ounce box vanilla cake mix (plus required ingredients)

3 cups quartered strawberries (about 1 pound)

¼ cup granulated sugar

Pinch of salt

2 pieces refrigerated pie dough (from one 14-ounce box)

All-purpose flour, for dusting

Coarse sugar, for sprinkling

We usually make our own pie dough, but the store-bought stuff actually works better for this cake-meets-pie: It's much sturdier.

1 Preheat the oven to 350°. Spray a pie plate with cooking spray. Make the cake batter according to the package directions; fill the pie plate three-quarters full. Bake just until the edges are set, 20 to 25 minutes.

2 Meanwhile, make the strawberry filling: Toss the strawberries, granulated sugar and salt in a bowl. Let sit 20 minutes.

3 Unroll 1 piece of pie dough on a lightly floured cutting board. Cut into 1-inch-wide strips with a knife for the lattice-top crust. Set aside.

4 Unroll the remaining piece of pie dough. Cut three 1-inch-wide strips from the middle of the round and press the strips together, end to end, to form 1 long strip. (This will be used for the piecrust edge.)

5 Transfer the partially baked cake to a rack; let cool slightly. Drain the strawberry mixture and spoon it onto the cake, pressing the berries into the top. Increase the oven temperature to 450°.

6 Arrange half of the pie dough strips for the top crust in parallel rows over the strawberries, about 1 inch apart, using the shorter strips on the ends.

7 Fold back every other strip halfway. Lay a new strip across the center of the pie as shown; unfold the folded strips over the new one. Repeat to create the lattice top.

8 Trim the edges, then drape the long dough strip around the rim; trim and press the ends together. Tuck the edge of the dough under itself, then crimp with your fingers.

9 Sprinkle the crust with coarse sugar and return the cake to the oven. Bake until golden, 10 to 15 more minutes. (Cover the edge with foil if it browns too quickly.)

CARROT CAKE

SERVES 8 TO 10

ACTIVE: 45 min

TOTAL: 45 min

- 1 16-ounce frozen pound cake, thawed slightly
- 1 16-ounce tub vanilla frosting
- 24 drops yellow food coloring
- 6 drops red food coloring
- 4 cups orange jelly beans
- 1 5-ounce bag green apple sour straws

You'll need a whopping 4 cups of orange jelly beans for this cake! Buy them in bulk at a candy store or search for "bulk jelly beans" online.

1 Trim 1 short end of the pound cake (discard the end), then cut a wedge off each side as shown.

2 Attach the wedges to each other with some of the frosting (crust sides together), then attach to the trimmed cake.

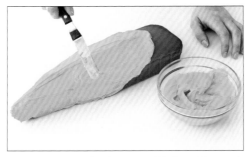

3 Mix the remaining frosting with the yellow and red food colorings. Spread over the cake.

4 Arrange the jelly beans on the cake in tight rows, covering the cake completely.

5 Trim the sour straws to various lengths and snip at an angle on the ends.

6 Gently stick the sour straw pieces into the top of the cake to form the carrot top.

PEANUT BUTTER AND JELLY SANDWICH CAKE

SERVES 8 TO 10

ACTIVE: 25 min

TOTAL: 55 min

1 stick unsalted butter, at room temperature, plus more for the pan

All-purpose flour, for dusting

1 16-to-18-ounce box white cake mix (plus required ingredients)

1 cup creamy peanut butter

2 cups confectioners' sugar

3 tablespoons milk

¾ cup grape jelly

A standard 9-inch-square cake pan is all you need to make this giant PB&J. Trim the top of the cake, but leave the browned edges—they look like crust!

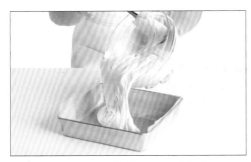

1 Preheat the oven to 350°. Butter a 9-inch-square pan, line with parchment, butter again and dust with flour. Make the cake batter according to the package directions and fill the pan three-quarters full (you may have batter left). Bake until a toothpick comes out clean, 30 to 35 minutes.

2 Let the cake cool in the pan 10 minutes, then turn out onto a rack and let cool completely. Transfer the cake to a work surface. Trim off the top using a serrated knife, then slice the cake in half horizontally.

3 Beat the butter and peanut butter with a mixer until smooth. Alternate adding the confectioners' sugar and milk, beating after each addition, until the frosting is fluffy and smooth. In another bowl, whisk the grape jelly until it is loose and spreadable.

4 Spread a thick layer of peanut butter frosting on the bottom cake half.

5 Spread the grape jelly on top of the peanut butter frosting, making sure it reaches the edges. Top with the remaining cake layer.

6 Cut the cake in half diagonally and transfer to a serving plate. Separate the halves slightly to show the filling.

TIKI COCKTAIL CAKE

SERVES 8 TO 10

ACTIVE: 45 min

TOTAL: 1 hr 20 min (plus freezing)

Cooking spray

1 16-to-18-ounce box chocolate cake mix

4 large eggs

1 cup buttermilk

½ cup vegetable oil

1 16-ounce tub milk chocolate frosting

¾ cup vanilla frosting

1½ cups sweetened shredded coconut, toasted

Dried fruit, for garnish

Mixing bowls can double as cake pans when you need a rounded shape; we used two small bowls plus a 6-inch cake pan to create this cocktail cake. Just make sure the bowls are labeled oven-safe.

1 Preheat the oven to 350°. Spray one 6-inch-round cake pan and two 1-quart ovenproof bowls with cooking spray. Beat the cake mix, eggs, buttermilk and vegetable oil with a mixer.

2 Divide the batter evenly among the pan and bowls; bake until a toothpick comes out clean, about 25 minutes for the pan and about 35 minutes for the bowls. Let cool; unmold.

3 Trim all 3 cakes to make them level. Hollow out the smaller end of 1 of the bowl cakes, carving about 1 inch deep. (Leave a thick rim around the edges.)

4 Put the uncarved bowl cake, wider side up, on a cake board or plate. Spread with a layer of chocolate frosting, then position the round cake on top.

5 Spread the round cake with chocolate frosting, then put the other bowl cake on top, carved part up. Freeze the cake about 1 hour (this will make it easier to frost).

6 Frost the outer rim and inside of the hole with vanilla frosting (an offset spatula works best). Put the remaining vanilla frosting in a resealable plastic bag.

7 Spread the remaining chocolate frosting over the outside of the cake. Press handfuls of toasted coconut into the frosting, covering the cake completely.

8 Microwave the bag of vanilla frosting for 5 seconds (the bag will not melt). Snip off a corner and squeeze the frosting into the top of the cake so it looks like liquid.

9 Thread dried fruit onto a wooden skewer and insert it into the cake. Add a cocktail umbrella and straw.

CHEESEBURGER CAKE

SERVES 14 TO 16

ACTIVE: 45 min

TOTAL: 1 hr 30 min

Cooking spray

2 16-to-18-ounce boxes chocolate cake mix

8 large eggs

2 cups buttermilk

1 cup vegetable oil

¼ cup green decorating sugar or granulated sugar

8 spearmint leaf gummy candies

3 ounces orange rolled fondant

Cornstarch, for dusting

1 16-ounce tub vanilla frosting

1 16-ounce tub chocolate frosting

¾ teaspoon yellow food coloring

5 drops red food coloring

2 tablespoons crispy rice cereal

Gummy candies are perfect for cake decorating: You can roll them out and fold, cut or shape them to look like anything—check out the lettuce on this faux burger!

1 Preheat the oven to 350°. Spray a 2½-quart ovenproof bowl and two 8-inch-round cake pans with cooking spray. Beat the cake mix, eggs, buttermilk and vegetable oil in a large bowl with a mixer.

2 Divide the batter among the bowl and pans; bake until a toothpick comes out clean, about 25 minutes for the pans and about 45 minutes for the bowl. Let cool 15 minutes, then unmold onto racks.

3 Make the lettuce: Sprinkle some green or white sugar on a cutting board. Roll out the spearmint candies with a rolling pin until thin and flat, sprinkling with more sugar to keep the candies from sticking.

4 Cut each flattened gummy piece into 3 strips. Fold each strip accordion-style to make ruffles; pinch the ends together.

5 Make the cheese: Roll out the orange fondant on a cornstarch-dusted surface to about ⅛ inch thick. Trim the fondant into a 7-inch square; cover with plastic wrap and set aside.

6 Trim 1 round cake and the flat side of the bowl cake until level; save the trimmings. Mix the vanilla frosting, ¼ cup chocolate frosting and the yellow and red food colorings to make a light brown frosting.

7 Make the bottom bun: Put the trimmed round cake on a serving plate or cake board. Frost with light brown frosting. Arrange the gummy-candy ruffles around the edge of the cake.

8 Make the patty: Spread the remaining chocolate frosting over the top and sides of the untrimmed round cake. Crumble the cake trimmings; press into the frosting.

9 Put the chocolate patty on the bottom bun; drape the orange fondant on top. Frost the bowl-shaped cake with light brown frosting; place on the patty. Press the rice cereal into the frosting.

STEAK FRITES CAKE

MAKES 4 PLATES (SERVES 8)

ACTIVE: 30 min

TOTAL: 1 hr 10 min

FOR THE STEAKS

- 1 1½-quart cylindrical carton chocolate ice cream
- ½ cup finely crushed chocolate wafer cookies

FOR THE FRIES

- 2 12-ounce frozen pound cakes, thawed slightly
- 1 stick unsalted butter, melted
- ½ cup seedless strawberry jam

You can use a regular knife to cut the pound cake into "fries," but a crinkle cutter is much more fun. Buy one for this and you'll definitely use it again: It's a great way to cut fruit and veggies for kids!

1 Make the steaks: Using a serrated knife, slice the carton of ice cream crosswise into 4 rounds, dipping the knife in hot water as needed. Snip off the carton with kitchen shears.

2 Tightly wrap each ice cream round in plastic wrap, then form into a steak shape with your hands (the warmth of your hands will soften the ice cream). Freeze until firm, about 30 minutes.

3 Unwrap 1 ice cream steak and transfer to a piece of parchment or wax paper. Dip a metal skewer in hot water, then press into the ice cream to create parallel diagonal grill-mark lines.

4 Make lines in the opposite direction to form a crosshatch pattern, dipping the skewer in hot water as needed.

5 Fill the lines with the chocolate cookie crumbs. Transfer the steak to a baking sheet and freeze until firm, about 30 minutes. Repeat with the remaining ice cream steaks.

6 Make the fries: Preheat the oven to 350°. Using a crinkle vegetable cutter or a chef's knife, trim the sides of the pound cakes, then cut each cake crosswise into ¼-inch-thick slices.

7 Cut each cake slice into sticks. Divide between 2 parchment-lined rimmed baking sheets.

8 Drizzle the melted butter over the pound cake fries and toss. Bake until lightly toasted, about 8 minutes, tossing halfway through. Let the fries cool slightly.

9 Arrange the ice cream steaks, the pound cake fries and strawberry jam on plates. Each plate serves 2.

SPAGHETTI AND MEATBALLS CAKE

SERVES 10 TO 12

ACTIVE: 1 hr

TOTAL: 2 hr

1 16-to-18-ounce box chocolate cake mix (plus required ingredients)

2 16-ounce tubs vanilla frosting

3 drops yellow food coloring

½ teaspoon cocoa powder

1 16-ounce bag frozen strawberries, thawed

White chocolate, for grating

Turn this cake into a fun birthday party project and let kids decorate their own miniature versions. Give everyone a cupcake and a small resealable plastic bag of pale yellow frosting, then put out bowls of cake "meatballs" and strawberry "sauce" for the top.

1 Make two 8-inch-round chocolate cakes as the cake mix label directs; let cool completely. Crumble 1 cake into a bowl. Squeeze a handful of crumbs into a 2-inch ball; roll between your hands until smooth. Repeat to make 2 more balls.

2 Sprinkle some of the remaining cake crumbs on a clean surface. One at a time, roll the cake balls in the crumbs, pressing lightly to coat. If necessary, moisten the cake balls with water to help the crumbs stick.

3 Assemble the cake: Put the remaining whole cake on a serving plate or cake board. Spread about 1½ cups vanilla frosting on the cake with an offset spatula; run the spatula around the sides to make it smooth.

4 Arrange the cake balls on the cake. Mix the remaining frosting, the yellow food coloring and cocoa in a bowl; transfer to a pastry bag with a small round tip and pipe around the cake balls to look like spaghetti.

5 Make the strawberry sauce: Puree the strawberries in a food processor until slightly smooth with a few chunks. Spoon some of the puree around the meatballs to look like sauce.

6 Grate white chocolate on top of the cake to look like parmesan cheese. Serve the cake with the remaining strawberry puree on the side.

CANDY BAR CAKE

SERVES 10 TO 12

ACTIVE: 45 min

TOTAL: 2 hr

The "nougat" layer of this super-size candy bar is chocolate frosting—and it's super rich, so serve the cake in thin slices!

FOR THE CAKE

- 1 11-ounce frozen pound cake, thawed slightly
- 3 ounces semisweet chocolate, finely chopped
- 1½ sticks (12 tablespoons) unsalted butter, at room temperature
- 3 tablespoons milk
- 1 1-pound box confectioners' sugar
- ¾ cup salted roasted peanuts
- 2 cups dulce de leche

FOR THE COATING

- 10 ounces semisweet chocolate, finely chopped
- 1 stick cold unsalted butter, cut into pieces

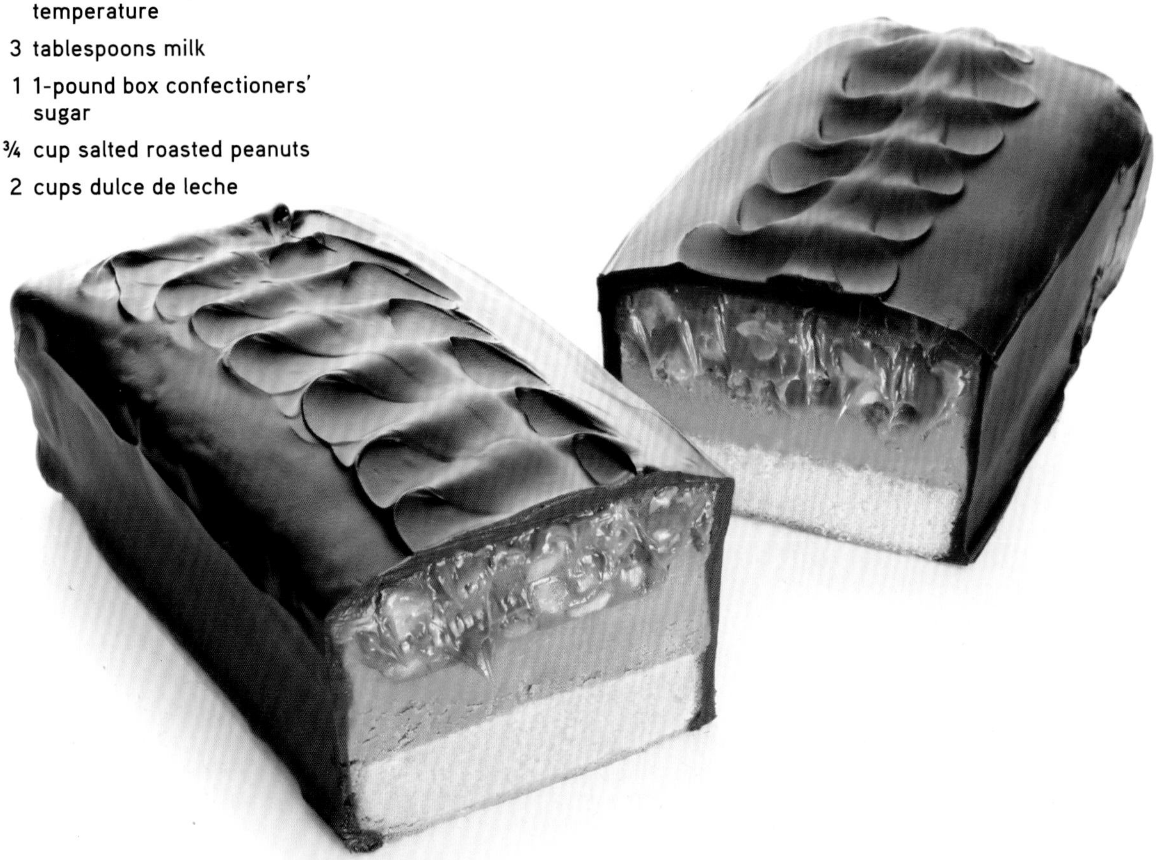

1 Assemble the cake: Trim ½ inch off the short ends of the pound cake, then trim the domed top to make it flat. Stand the cake on its side and slice in half horizontally to make two equal-size rectangles.

2 Microwave the chocolate in 30-second intervals, stirring, to melt. Beat the butter, milk and confectioners' sugar; beat in the melted chocolate. Add more milk, if needed, until spreadable.

3 Lay the cake halves on a rack set on a rimmed baking sheet. Spread frosting on one short end of each cake; press together to form a long rectangle. (Slide some cardboard underneath to move the cake later.)

4 Spread the remaining frosting on the cake in a 1-inch-thick layer, making the edges slightly higher than the center. Smooth the top and sides with an offset spatula. Freeze until firm, about 30 minutes.

5 Mix the peanuts and dulce de leche in a bowl.

6 Spread the peanut mixture on the frosting in a flat, even layer. Freeze until the dulce de leche is firm, about 30 minutes.

7 Meanwhile, make the chocolate coating: Microwave the chocolate and butter in 30-second intervals, stirring, until melted and smooth.

8 Pour the chocolate on the cake and spread it evenly over the top and sides with an offset spatula. Freeze until the chocolate cools slightly, 6 to 8 minutes.

9 Starting at a short end of the cake, dip the edge of an offset spatula into the chocolate at an angle and pull up, repeating to create a wave pattern on top. Refrigerate 10 minutes before serving.

CHEESE WHEEL CAKE

SERVES 10 TO 12

ACTIVE: 1 hr

TOTAL: 2 hr

The red fondant "rind" on this gouda cake is edible, but like a real wax rind, you can remove it before eating if you'd like.

Cooking spray

1 16-to-18-ounce box yellow cake mix (plus required ingredients)

1 16-ounce tub plus 1 cup vanilla frosting

1 bunch seedless grapes, cut into clusters

1 large pasteurized egg white, lightly beaten

¾ cup granulated sugar

Confectioners' sugar, for dusting

1 24-ounce package red rolled fondant

Yellow food coloring

1 to 2 tablespoons vegetable oil

Butter cookies, for serving

1 Preheat the oven to 350°. Line two 9-inch-round cake pans with wax paper or parchment and coat with cooking spray. Prepare the cake batter as the label directs; divide between the pans. Bake as directed.

2 Let the cakes cool 15 minutes in the pans, then remove to a rack and let cool completely. Using a small serrated knife, trim the top edges of each cake at an angle to give it a rounded shape.

3 Put 1 cake layer on wax paper or parchment, trimmed-side down. Spread with frosting; top with the other cake layer, trimmed-side up. Cover the whole cake with frosting, reserving 1 cup. Freeze 30 minutes.

4 Meanwhile, make the sugared grapes: Brush the grapes with the beaten egg white, then spoon the granulated sugar on top. Let dry at least 1 hour at room temperature.

5 Dust a work surface with confectioners' sugar. Roll out one-quarter of the fondant until about ⅛ inch thick, dusting with more confectioners' sugar as needed.

6 Cut out an 8-inch circle of fondant and place on a sheet of wax paper or parchment. Place the cake on top.

7 Add the scraps to the remaining fondant and roll out into a 13-inch circle, about ⅛ inch thick. Drape the fondant over the cake to cover completely.

8 Smooth the fondant with your hands and tuck it in at the base of the cake; trim the excess with a knife. Cut out a wedge of the cake.

9 Tint the reserved 1 cup frosting pale yellow with the food coloring; spread on the cut sides of the cake. Rub the vegetable oil all over the fondant. Arrange on a board with the cookies and grapes.

FLOWERPOT CAKE

SERVES 10 TO 12

ACTIVE: 1 hr
TOTAL: 2 hr

You can eat this whole terra-cotta pot—including the flowers! Look for edible flowers at farmers' markets (we used nasturtiums and pansies), or order them online.

Cooking spray

1 16-to-18-ounce box devil's food cake mix (plus required ingredients)

1 16-ounce tub plus 1 cup milk chocolate frosting

3 tablespoons unsweetened cocoa powder, plus more for dusting

1 24-ounce package white rolled fondant

¾ teaspoon red gel food coloring

¼ teaspoon orange gel food coloring

Mint sprigs and edible flowers, for topping

1 Preheat the oven to 350°. Line a 6-inch-round and an 8-inch-round cake pan with parchment; coat with cooking spray. Prepare the cake batter as directed; divide between the pans and bake 25 to 30 minutes.

2 Level the cake tops with a serrated knife (save the trimmings). Halve the cakes horizontally; stack on a cake board with the 8-inch layers on the bottom, spreading frosting between each layer.

3 Hold a serrated knife at an angle and trim the edges of the cake all the way around to make an upside-down pot shape. Cover the cake with all but ½ cup of the remaining frosting; freeze 30 minutes.

4 Sprinkle 3 tablespoons cocoa powder on a sheet of parchment; put the fondant on top, make a small well in the middle and put the red and orange food coloring in the well. Knead until the color is even.

5 Dust a surface with cocoa powder; roll out the colored fondant into a 24-by-6½-inch rectangle, trimming the edges to make them straight. Cut off a 24-by-1¼-inch strip of fondant; set aside.

6 Wrap the wide piece of fondant around the cake, pressing and smoothing it with your fingers. Trim the excess with a paring knife.

7 Reroll the fondant scraps and cut out a 5-inch circle; press the fondant circle on top of the cake to form the pot bottom. Invert the cake onto a board or plate.

8 Lightly brush the thin strip of fondant with water; wrap it around the top edge of the cake, allowing the strip to come slightly above the edge. Trim the ends.

9 Cover the top of the cake with the remaining ½ cup frosting, then crumble the cake trimmings on top. When ready to serve, add mint sprigs and edible flowers.

GUACAMOLE AND CHIPS CAKE

SERVES 10 TO 12

ACTIVE: 45 min

TOTAL: 1 hr 50 min (plus freezing)

Cooking spray

1 16-to-18-ounce box chocolate cake mix (plus required ingredients)

1 16-ounce tub chocolate frosting

12 chocolate sandwich cookies, ground in a food processor

1 pint vanilla ice cream, softened

Green, yellow and red food colorings

¼ cup red and/or green candied cherries, chopped

Cinnamon-sugar pita chips, for serving

This looks like a traditional Mexican mortar (called a molcajete), but it's actually a crumb-covered chocolate cake sitting on three chocolate cupcakes—and the "guacamole" is green-tinted ice cream! Serve it with cinnamon-sugar pita chips.

1 Preheat the oven to 350°. Spray a 2½-quart ovenproof bowl with cooking spray. Prepare the cake mix as directed. Fill three cupcake liners two-thirds full with batter; pour the remaining batter into the bowl.

2 Bake the cupcakes and bowl cake until done, about 18 minutes for the cupcakes and 50 minutes for the bowl. Let cool. Unmold the bowl cake and peel off the cupcake liners. Freeze 20 minutes.

3 Put the bowl cake upright on a cake board or plate. Carve out the middle, about 1 inch from the edge, with a paring knife to make room for the "guacamole."

4 Cover the top and sides of the bowl cake with some of the chocolate frosting.

5 Pat the ground chocolate sandwich cookies over the frosting to cover. Invert the cake onto another cake board or plate.

6 Frost the bottom of the bowl cake. Trim the cupcake tops to make them level and attach to the bottom of the bowl cake with frosting.

7 Frost the sides of the cupcakes as shown. Pat cookie crumbs into the frosting to cover completely. Transfer to the freezer.

8 Mix the ice cream with the green, yellow and red food colorings until it turns guacamole green. Stir in the chopped candied cherries.

9 Invert the cake so it's bowl-side up. Pat any loose crumbs into place, then fill with the ice cream. Freeze at least 1 hour. Serve with cinnamon-sugar pita chips.

POPCORN CAKE

SERVES 10 TO 12

ACTIVE: 45 min

TOTAL: 1 hr 30 min

1 16-to-18-ounce box yellow cake mix (plus required ingredients)

4 cups vanilla frosting

Cornstarch, for dusting

This is a great cake for movie night or an Oscars party. Be careful when you attach the red fondant strips: The color can bleed if you use too much water.

1 Prepare the cake mix as the label directs for a 9-by-13-inch cake; bake and let cool. Cut in half crosswise. Spread some of the frosting on one half, then top with the second half. Cover the layer cake with frosting.

2 Dust a flat surface with cornstarch. Using a rolling pin, roll out the white fondant to at least 16 by 18 inches (about ⅛ inch thick).

3 Drape the white fondant over the cake, covering the cake but leaving one short end exposed with a slight overhang, as shown. Smooth the fondant, then cut away any excess, except for the overhang.

4 Roll out the red fondant on a cornstarch-dusted surface until very thin. Cut into about 15 strips, ½ by 14 inches each.

5 One at a time, spread a little bit of water on the back of each red fondant strip with your finger and attach to the cake, trimming as needed. (Do not use too much water; the red dye will bleed.)

6 Press some of the caramel corn onto the uncovered side of the cake. Continue adding caramel corn until the cake looks like an overflowing bag. Use more frosting to stick the pieces together.

LOBSTER ROLL CAKE

SERVES 6

ACTIVE: 25 min
TOTAL: 25 min

- 1 cup coarsely chopped strawberries
- 1 cup mini marshmallows
- ⅓ cup sweetened shredded coconut
- ½ cup plain Greek yogurt
- ½ cup whipped cream
- 2 pieces green apple licorice
- 1 11-ounce frozen pound cake, thawed
- 2 gummy lemon slices

This fake-out lobster roll looks even more like the real thing if you serve it in a classic paper basket. Search for "large paper food trays" online.

1 Combine the strawberries, mini marshmallows, coconut, yogurt and whipped cream in a large bowl with a rubber spatula.

2 Using kitchen shears, cut the green licorice on the diagonal into small pieces. Fold into the strawberry mixture; cover and refrigerate.

3 Preheat the broiler. Using a serrated knife, shave the edges off both long sides of the cake.

4 Make 2 lengthwise cuts, about 1 inch deep, in the top of the cake, 1 inch in from each edge.

5 Carefully pry out the middle strip. Place the rest of the cake on a baking sheet and broil, turning, until toasted on all sides.

6 Fill the opening in the cake with the strawberry mixture, mounding it on top; serve with the gummy lemon slices.

SHOW-OFF CAKES

BOSTON CREAM PIE

SERVES 8 TO 10

ACTIVE: 1 hr
TOTAL: 2 hr (plus chilling)

FOR THE CAKE

Unsalted butter, for the pan
1¼ cups cake flour
1 teaspoon baking powder
¼ teaspoon salt
4 large eggs, at room temperature
1 cup sugar
½ cup whole milk
⅓ cup vegetable oil
1½ teaspoons vanilla extract

FOR THE PUDDING

1½ cups whole milk
2 teaspoons vanilla extract
2 large eggs plus 4 egg yolks
½ cup sugar
¼ cup cornstarch
Pinch of salt

FOR THE GLAZE

4 ounces semisweet chocolate, finely chopped
½ cup heavy cream
1 teaspoon vanilla extract
Pinch of salt

Cake flour makes this cake extra soft. In a pinch, you can substitute 1 cup plus 2 tablespoons all-purpose flour, plus 2 tablespoons cornstarch.

1 Preheat the oven to 350°. Butter a 9-inch-round cake pan and line the bottom with parchment paper. Make the cake: Sift the flour, baking powder and salt into a large bowl. Beat the eggs and sugar in a stand mixer fitted with the whisk attachment on high speed until pale and tripled in volume, about 15 minutes. Gently fold in the flour mixture in 2 additions using a rubber spatula, scraping down the bowl.

2 Add the milk, vegetable oil and vanilla and beat with the mixer until combined. Pour the batter into the prepared pan and bake until a toothpick inserted into the center comes out clean, 25 to 30 minutes. Transfer the pan to a rack and let cool 10 minutes, then invert the cake onto the rack. Invert again and let cool completely.

3 Meanwhile, make the pudding: Heat the milk and vanilla in a medium saucepan over medium heat (do not boil). Whisk the whole eggs, egg yolks and sugar in a large bowl until light and fluffy. Add the cornstarch and salt and whisk vigorously until no lumps remain. Whisk about ¼ cup of the hot milk mixture into the egg mixture, then gradually whisk in the remaining hot milk mixture.

4 Pour the egg-milk mixture into the saucepan and cook over low heat, whisking constantly, until thick and pudding-like, 10 to 15 minutes. Strain through a fine-mesh sieve into a bowl, using a rubber spatula to push the pudding through. Let cool slightly, stirring occasionally. Press plastic wrap directly onto the surface and refrigerate at least 2 hours.

5 Slice the cake in half horizontally with a long serrated knife. Place the bottom half of the cake cut-side up on a platter. Top with the pudding, spreading it to about ¼ inch from the edges. Carefully place the other cake half on top, cut-side down, pressing gently.

6 Make the glaze: Heat the chocolate, cream, vanilla and salt in a saucepan over medium-low heat, stirring, until melted and smooth, about 2 minutes. Let cool about 5 minutes, then pour over the cake and smooth with an offset spatula. Refrigerate at least 30 minutes or up to 4 hours before serving.

BOURBON PRALINE CAKE

SERVES 8

ACTIVE: 40 min

TOTAL: 2 hr 10 min

FOR THE PRALINE LAYER

- 4 tablespoons unsalted butter, plus more for the pan
- ⅓ cup packed light brown sugar
- ⅓ cup light corn syrup
- ¼ teaspoon kosher salt
- 1½ teaspoons vanilla extract
- 2¼ cups pecans, toasted

FOR THE CAKE

- 1½ cups cake flour
- 1 teaspoon baking soda
- ¼ teaspoon ground nutmeg
- ¼ teaspoon fine salt
- ⅓ cup buttermilk, at room temperature
- 2 tablespoons bourbon
- 1½ sticks (12 tablespoons) unsalted butter, at room temperature
- 1¼ cups granulated sugar
- 3 large eggs, at room temperature
- ½ cup pecans, toasted and chopped

The pecan layer is thick and sticky, so you'll need to line the whole pan with parchment. Use a circle of parchment for the bottom of the pan and a separate strip for the side.

1 Preheat the oven to 350°. Butter a 9-inch springform pan, then line the bottom and sides with parchment paper and butter the paper. Wrap the outside of the pan with foil.

2 Make the praline layer: Melt the butter in a saucepan over medium heat. Whisk in the brown sugar, corn syrup, kosher salt and vanilla. Spread in the prepared pan and scatter the pecans on top; set aside.

3 Make the cake: Whisk the flour, baking soda, nutmeg and fine salt in a large bowl. Whisk the buttermilk and bourbon in another bowl.

4 Beat the butter and granulated sugar with a mixer on medium-high speed until fluffy, 10 minutes. With the mixer on low, beat in the eggs, one at a time. Add the flour mixture in 3 parts, alternating with the buttermilk mixture, starting and ending with flour. Fold in the pecans.

5 Pour the batter into the prepared pan and bake until a toothpick inserted into the center comes out clean, about 1 hour. Cool on a rack, 30 minutes. Remove the springform ring, invert the cake onto a plate and remove the paper.

LEMON-CRANBERRY BUNDT CAKE

SERVES 8 TO 12

ACTIVE: 50 min

TOTAL: 2 hr (plus overnight resting)

FOR THE CAKE

- 3¼ sticks unsalted butter, cubed, at room temperature, plus more for the pan
- 3 cups cake flour, sifted, plus more for the pan
- 1 12-ounce bag cranberries, thawed if frozen
- 2½ cups granulated sugar
- 6 tablespoons whole milk
- 4 large eggs plus 2 egg yolks
- 2 teaspoons vanilla extract
- 2 tablespoons finely grated lemon zest
- 1½ teaspoons baking powder
- ½ teaspoon salt

FOR THE SYRUP AND GLAZE

- ¼ cup granulated sugar
- ½ cup plus 2 tablespoons Meyer lemon juice (or use a mix of regular lemon juice and orange juice)
- 1½ cups confectioners' sugar

To make sugared cranberries for the plate, dip whole berries in a beaten pasteurized egg white, toss with sugar and let dry on parchment paper.

1 Make the cake: Preheat the oven to 350°. Butter and flour a 10-cup fluted Bundt pan. Cook the cranberries with ¾ cup granulated sugar in a pot over medium-high heat until juicy and the mixture reduces to about 1¼ cups, about 15 minutes. Let cool.

2 Whisk the milk, whole eggs and yolks, and vanilla in a medium bowl; set aside. Whisk the 3 cups flour, the remaining 1¾ cups granulated sugar, the lemon zest, baking powder and salt in a large bowl. Add the cubed 3¼ sticks butter and beat with a mixer on low speed until moistened. Add half of the milk mixture, increase the speed to medium and beat 1 minute. Add the remaining milk mixture in 2 batches, beating between each addition. Scrape down the sides of the bowl and beat again, about 30 seconds.

3 Transfer two-thirds of the batter to the pan. Spoon the cranberry mixture in a ring around the middle of the batter (don't let it touch the pan). Top with the remaining batter and smooth evenly. Bake until a toothpick inserted into the center comes out clean, 55 to 60 minutes.

4 Meanwhile, make the syrup: Dissolve the ¼ cup granulated sugar in ½ cup lemon juice in a saucepan over low heat. Remove the cake from the oven, poke the surface all over with a skewer and pour the syrup on top. Let cool 10 minutes in the pan. Carefully invert the cake onto a parchment-lined rack to cool completely. Wrap tightly in plastic wrap and let sit overnight.

5 When ready to serve, whisk the confectioners' sugar and the remaining 2 tablespoons lemon juice until smooth. Spoon over the cake.

CARAMEL APPLE UPSIDE-DOWN CAKE

SERVES 8 TO 10

ACTIVE: 1 hr
TOTAL: 2 hr 50 min

FOR THE CARAMEL AND APPLES

- 4 tablespoons unsalted butter, plus more for the pan
- 3 cups sugar
- 5 tablespoons light corn syrup
- 1 cup heavy cream
- 4 large Golden Delicious apples (1¾ to 2 pounds)

FOR THE BATTER

- 3 cups all-purpose flour
- 2 teaspoons baking powder
- ½ teaspoon baking soda
- 1 teaspoon salt
- ½ teaspoon ground cinnamon
- ½ cup sour cream
- ⅓ cup fresh orange juice
- 1 tablespoon vanilla extract
- 1 stick unsalted butter, at room temperature
- 1½ cups sugar
- 3 large eggs

You'll need a 3-inch-deep pan for this cake. If you don't have one, measure your springform pan—it might be deep enough.

1 Butter a 9-by-3-inch round cake pan. Make the caramel: Cook the sugar and corn syrup in a skillet over medium-high heat, stirring occasionally, until dark amber, 7 to 10 minutes. Reduce the heat to medium. Add the cream and 4 tablespoons butter (be careful; it will splatter) and cook, stirring, 3 minutes. Remove from the heat and let sit 1 minute. Pour 1½ cups caramel into a glass measuring cup and set aside. Pour the remaining caramel into the prepared pan.

2 Cut 3 apples into quarters and remove the cores. Arrange the pieces skin-side down in the pan, overlapping slightly, to form a ring about ½ inch from the edge. Chop any leftover slices into small pieces. Halve the remaining whole apple crosswise and scoop out the seeds; leave the stem. Chop the bottom half and add to the other pieces. Arrange the apple top, stem-side down, in the center of the pan.

3 Preheat the oven to 350°. Make the batter: Whisk the flour, baking powder, baking soda, salt and cinnamon in a bowl. In a small bowl, whisk the sour cream, orange juice and vanilla. Using a mixer, beat the butter and sugar on medium-high speed until fluffy, about 5 minutes. Add the eggs, one at a time, and beat until pale and creamy, 5 more minutes. Scrape down the bowl with a rubber spatula. With the mixer on low, add the sour cream mixture in 2 batches, alternating with the flour mixture in 2 batches. Turn off the mixer and scrape down the bowl; finish combining the batter by hand.

4 Spread the batter over the apples in the pan and top with the chopped apples. Bake on the middle rack until the cake springs back when pressed, 1 hour to 1 hour, 20 minutes. Let cool in the pan on a rack.

5 Bring 1 inch of water to a simmer in a wide skillet. Run a sharp knife around the inside of the pan a few times, then rest the pan in the water to soften the caramel, 8 minutes. Dry the pan, then invert a plate on top of the cake and flip the plate and cake over; using pot holders, wriggle the pan off. Soften the reserved 1½ cups caramel in the microwave, 2 minutes, and drizzle onto the cake; serve any extra sauce on the side.

BLUEBERRY BUTTERMILK BUNDT CAKE

SERVES 10

ACTIVE: 1 hr

TOTAL: 2 hr 30 min (plus cooling)

FOR THE CAKE

2 sticks unsalted butter, at room temperature, plus more for the pan

3 cups plus 2 tablespoons all-purpose flour

2½ teaspoons baking powder

1¼ teaspoons salt

1¾ cups granulated sugar

¼ cup vegetable oil

4 large eggs, at room temperature

1 teaspoon vanilla extract

¾ cup buttermilk

2 cups blueberries (about 1 pint)

FOR THE TOPPINGS

2 to 3 cups large strawberries, halved or quartered

1 to 2 tablespoons granulated sugar

2½ cups confectioners' sugar

1 tablespoon unsalted butter, at room temperature

4 to 5 tablespoons milk

To prevent the blueberries from sinking to the bottom of the cake, toss them in flour before adding them to the batter.

1 Make the cake: Preheat the oven to 350°. Generously butter a nonstick 12-cup Bundt pan. Whisk 3 cups flour, the baking powder and salt in a medium bowl.

2 Beat 2 sticks butter, the granulated sugar and vegetable oil in a bowl with a mixer on medium-high speed until fluffy, at least 5 minutes, scraping down the sides of the bowl with a rubber spatula as needed. Reduce the mixer speed to low; beat in the eggs, one at a time, then beat in the vanilla. Add about one-third of the flour mixture and half of the buttermilk; beat until almost incorporated. Add another one-third of the flour mixture and the remaining buttermilk. Beat, scraping down the sides of the bowl as needed, until just combined. Add the remaining flour mixture and beat 30 seconds. Finish incorporating the flour by hand to avoid overmixing.

3 Toss the blueberries with the remaining 2 tablespoons flour in a small bowl. Spoon one-third of the batter evenly into the prepared pan. Sprinkle in half of the blueberries, then top with another one-third of the batter. Scatter the remaining blueberries on top and cover with the rest of the batter; smooth the top. Bake until the cake is golden and a toothpick comes out clean, 1 hour to 1 hour, 10 minutes. Transfer to a rack and let cool 30 minutes in the pan. Run a sharp knife around the edges of the pan, then invert the cake onto the rack to cool completely.

4 Meanwhile, make the toppings: Toss the strawberries with the granulated sugar in a bowl; set aside to macerate, 30 minutes. Just before serving, make the glaze: Whisk the confectioners' sugar, butter and 4 tablespoons milk in a bowl (whisk in up to 1 more tablespoon of milk, a little at a time, if the glaze is too thick). Pour the glaze over the cake, letting it drip down the sides. Serve with the strawberries and their juices.

COCONUT ROULADE WITH RUM BUTTERCREAM

SERVES 10

ACTIVE: 1 hr 10 min

TOTAL: 1 hr 25 min (plus cooling)

FOR THE CAKE

Unsalted butter, for the pan

1 cup all-purpose flour, plus more for dusting

1½ cups granulated sugar

1 teaspoon baking powder

¾ teaspoon baking soda

¼ teaspoon salt

4 large eggs, separated, plus 2 egg whites, all at room temperature

½ cup vegetable oil

½ cup coconut milk

1½ teaspoons coconut extract

Pinch of cream of tartar

Confectioners' sugar

1 tablespoon white rum

FOR THE FROSTING

6 large egg whites

1 cup plus 2 tablespoons granulated sugar

3 sticks unsalted butter, cut into pieces, at room temperature

3 tablespoons white rum

4 cups sweetened shredded coconut

This frosting, called a Swiss meringue buttercream, is rich and glossy. It may look curdled when you add the butter, but keep beating and it will come together.

1 Make the cake: Preheat the oven to 350°. Butter an 11-by-17-inch rimmed baking sheet and line the bottom with parchment. Butter the parchment and dust with flour, tapping out the excess. Whisk 1 cup each flour and granulated sugar, the baking powder, baking soda and salt in a bowl. In a large bowl, whisk the 4 egg yolks, vegetable oil, coconut milk and coconut extract. Whisk in the flour mixture in 2 batches.

2 Beat the 6 egg whites and cream of tartar with a mixer on medium speed until foamy. Increase the speed to medium high; gradually add the remaining ½ cup granulated sugar and beat until stiff, shiny peaks form. Fold one-third of the beaten egg whites into the batter with a rubber spatula, then gently fold in the rest.

3 Spread the batter on the prepared baking sheet and bake until the cake is golden and springs back when pressed, 15 to 20 minutes. Loosen the edges of the cake with a knife; transfer the baking sheet to a rack and let the cake cool slightly. Dust a large piece of parchment paper with confectioners' sugar. Invert the cake onto the parchment and peel off the parchment on top. Brush the cake with the rum.

4 Make the frosting: Whisk the egg whites and granulated sugar in a heatproof bowl set over a saucepan of simmering water until the mixture is warm and the sugar dissolves (do not let the bowl touch the water). Remove the bowl; let cool slightly. Beat the egg white mixture with a mixer on medium-high speed until stiff peaks form, 12 minutes. Beat in the butter, a few pieces at a time, then continue beating until glossy and smooth, 5 to 7 more minutes. Beat in the rum.

5 Spread about 2 cups of the frosting on the cake; sprinkle with 2 cups coconut. Starting at a short end, roll up the cake, using the parchment to help you. Transfer to a platter, seam-side down. Cover the cake with the remaining frosting and sprinkle with the remaining coconut.

DULCE DE LECHE CRÊPE CAKE

SERVES 8

ACTIVE: 45 min

TOTAL: 1 hr 15 min

FOR THE CRÊPES

- 1½ cups whole milk
- 4 large eggs
- 1½ cups all-purpose flour
- ¼ cup unsweetened cocoa powder
- ¼ cup granulated sugar
- ¾ teaspoon vanilla extract
- ⅛ teaspoon kosher salt

  Unsalted butter, melted, for brushing

FOR THE FILLING AND TOPPING

- 2 sticks unsalted butter, at room temperature
- 2¾ cups plus 1 tablespoon confectioners' sugar
- 1 cup dulce de leche, plus more for drizzling
- 1 cup heavy cream

Don't worry if your first few crêpes are misshapen: It can take a couple tries to get them right.

1 Make the crêpes: Combine the milk, eggs, flour, cocoa powder, granulated sugar, vanilla and salt in a blender and process until smooth. Refrigerate the batter 30 minutes.

2 Lightly brush a 10-inch nonstick skillet with melted butter and place over medium heat. Add a scant ¼ cup of batter and quickly swirl the pan to coat the bottom. Cook until set on top and golden on the bottom, about 30 seconds. Carefully lift the edges of the crêpe with a rubber spatula, then flip with your fingers and cook 20 more seconds. Invert the crêpe onto a plate. Repeat with the remaining batter to make 14 to 18 crêpes, brushing the skillet with more butter as needed. Stack the finished crêpes on the plate and let cool completely.

3 Make the filling: Beat the butter in a stand mixer fitted with the paddle attachment on medium-high speed until light and fluffy. Add 2¾ cups confectioners' sugar in 2 batches, beating until smooth and fluffy. Add the dulce de leche and beat until combined.

4 Assemble the cake just before serving: Place 1 crêpe on a platter. Spread with a scant ¼ cup of the filling, then top with another crêpe. Repeat with the remaining filling and crêpes, ending with a crêpe on top.

5 Beat the heavy cream and the remaining 1 tablespoon confectioners' sugar with a mixer until stiff peaks form. Top the cake with the whipped cream and dulce de leche; serve immediately.

STRAWBERRY SHORTCAKE LAYER CAKE

SERVES 8

ACTIVE: 40 min

TOTAL: 1 hr 35 min

FOR THE CAKE

- 5 tablespoons unsalted butter, melted, plus more for the pan
- 1⅓ cups all-purpose flour, plus more for dusting
- 1¼ cups granulated sugar
- 1¼ teaspoons baking powder
- ½ teaspoon salt
- 1½ teaspoons vanilla bean paste (or seeds from ½ vanilla bean)
- 2 large eggs, at room temperature, beaten
- ¾ cup whole milk, at room temperature
- ½ teaspoon finely grated lemon zest

FOR THE TOPPINGS AND FILLING

- 1½ quarts strawberries, hulled
- 1 tablespoon strawberry jelly
- 3 tablespoons confectioners' sugar
- 1 tablespoon fresh lemon juice
- 1½ cups cold heavy cream
- ¼ teaspoon vanilla extract

The secret ingredient in this cake is vanilla bean paste: It adds serious vanilla flavor. Pick up a jar at a baking-supply store or order some online.

1 Preheat the oven to 350°. Butter an 8-inch-round cake pan, then line the bottom with parchment paper; butter the parchment and dust with flour, tapping out the excess.

2 Make the cake: Whisk the 1⅓ cups flour, the granulated sugar, baking powder and salt in a medium bowl until combined. Whisk the melted butter, vanilla bean paste, eggs, milk and lemon zest in a medium bowl until just smooth. Add the milk mixture to the flour-sugar mixture and stir with a wooden spoon until incorporated. Pour the batter into the prepared pan and bake until a toothpick inserted into the middle comes out clean, 35 to 40 minutes. Transfer to a rack and let cool 10 minutes in the pan, then turn out of the pan onto the rack and let cool completely. Remove the parchment.

3 Meanwhile, make the toppings and filling: Halve 16 strawberries. Whisk 1 tablespoon water and the strawberry jelly in a medium bowl until smooth. Add the halved strawberries and toss to coat; set aside. Thinly slice the remaining strawberries, then toss with 2 tablespoons confectioners' sugar and the lemon juice in another medium bowl; set aside. Beat the heavy cream, the remaining 1 tablespoon confectioners' sugar and the vanilla extract with a mixer on medium-high speed until soft peaks form. Refrigerate the whipped cream until ready to assemble.

4 Cut the cake in half horizontally with a serrated knife. Place the bottom half cut-side up on a platter. Drizzle the juices from the sliced berries over the cut sides of both cake halves. Fold a few tablespoons of the whipped cream into the sliced berries; spoon them over the bottom cake layer. Cover with the other cake layer cut-side down, then top with the remaining whipped cream. Top with the halved strawberries and their juices.

S'MORES CAKE

SERVES 8 TO 10

ACTIVE: 1 hr 10 min
TOTAL: 3 hr 10 min

FOR THE CAKE

    Cooking spray

1 cup unsweetened cocoa powder

2½ cups all-purpose flour

2 cups sugar

1½ teaspoons baking powder

1 teaspoon baking soda

1 teaspoon salt

3 large eggs, at room temperature

¾ cup vegetable oil

½ cup sour cream

2 teaspoons vanilla extract

FOR THE GANACHE

½ cup heavy cream

4 ounces semisweet chocolate, finely chopped

    Pinch of salt

½ teaspoon vanilla extract

FOR THE FILLING

8 graham crackers, crushed

2 tablespoons unsalted butter, melted

    Pinch of salt

    Vegetable oil

1 16-ounce container marshmallow cream

This over-the-top cake starts to ooze as it sits (like real s'mores!), so assemble it close to serving time.

1 Make the cake: Preheat the oven to 350°. Coat two 9-inch-round cake pans with cooking spray and line the bottoms with parchment. Whisk the cocoa powder and 1½ cups boiling water in a bowl until smooth; set aside. Whisk the flour, sugar, baking powder, baking soda and salt in a large bowl. Add the eggs, vegetable oil, sour cream and vanilla and beat with a mixer on medium speed until smooth. Reduce the mixer speed to low; beat in the cocoa mixture in a steady stream until just combined; finish mixing with a rubber spatula. (The batter will be thin.)

2 Divide the batter between the prepared pans and tap the pans on the countertop to help the batter settle. Bake until a toothpick inserted into the center comes out clean, 30 to 40 minutes. Transfer to racks and let cool 10 minutes, then run a knife around the edges of the pans and turn the cakes out onto the racks to cool completely. Remove the parchment and trim the tops of the cakes with a long serrated knife to make them level. (The cakes can be wrapped in plastic wrap and frozen for up to 2 weeks; unwrap and thaw at room temperature before assembling.)

3 Make the ganache: Heat the cream, chocolate and salt in a heatproof bowl set over a saucepan of simmering water, stirring occasionally, until smooth (don't let the bowl touch the water). Stir in the vanilla. Remove the bowl from the pan and set aside until the ganache is cool and thick but still pourable, about 1 hour.

4 Meanwhile, make the filling: Preheat the oven to 350°. Toss the graham cracker crumbs, melted butter and salt in a bowl. Spread on a baking sheet. Bake, stirring occasionally, until toasted, 8 to 10 minutes.

5 Assemble the cake: Using a long serrated knife, slice each cake layer in half horizontally. Place 1 cake half on a platter. Using a lightly oiled offset spatula or spoon, spread one-third of the marshmallow cream on top, stopping 1 inch from the edge (if the marshmallow cream is stiff, microwave 10 to 15 seconds). Sprinkle one-third of the graham cracker mixture over the marshmallow cream. Repeat to make 4 layers, ending with cake; reserve a few tablespoons of the graham cracker mixture. Pour the ganache over the cake, letting it drip down the sides. Sprinkle with the reserved graham cracker mixture.

TOWERING FLOURLESS CHOCOLATE CAKE

SERVES 8 TO 10

ACTIVE: 50 min

TOTAL: 1 hr 45 min

FOR THE CAKE

- 2½ sticks unsalted butter, cut into pieces, plus more for the pan
- 6 ounces bittersweet chocolate, chopped
- 6 ounces unsweetened chocolate, chopped
- 6 large eggs
- ¾ cup turbinado sugar
- Pinch of salt
- ½ cup stout beer (such as Guinness)
- 1 teaspoon vanilla extract

FOR THE MERINGUE

- 2 ounces semisweet chocolate, chopped
- 2 tablespoons unsalted butter
- 1 tablespoon light corn syrup
- 1 cup granulated sugar
- 3 large egg whites
- ¼ teaspoon cream of tartar
- Pinch of salt
- 2 teaspoons vanilla extract

To get this look, pile the meringue on top of the cake, then use the back of a spoon to pull the meringue into swirly peaks.

1 Make the cake: Preheat the oven to 325°. Butter the bottom and sides of a 9-inch springform pan and line the bottom with parchment. Put the bittersweet and unsweetened chocolates in a heatproof bowl and set over a saucepan of simmering water (don't let the bowl touch the water). Stir until the chocolate melts; remove the bowl and set aside.

2 Put the eggs, turbinado sugar and salt in the bowl of a stand mixer. Set the bowl over the same pan of simmering water and whisk until the mixture is warm, about 2 minutes. Transfer the bowl to the stand mixer; beat with the whisk attachment on medium speed until tripled in volume, about 5 minutes.

3 Meanwhile, bring the beer and vanilla to a low boil in a saucepan. Reduce the mixer speed to low; beat in the beer mixture, then the melted chocolate, until combined, about 2 minutes. Gradually beat in the butter until incorporated. Pour the batter into the prepared pan and bake until a toothpick comes out with a few crumbs, about 35 minutes. Cool 1 hour in the pan on a rack, then run a knife around the edge of the pan and remove the ring. Let cool completely.

4 Make the meringue: Microwave the chocolate, butter and corn syrup in a microwave-safe bowl in 30-second intervals, stirring, until the chocolate melts.

5 Whisk the granulated sugar, egg whites, cream of tartar, salt and ⅓ cup water in a heatproof bowl. Put the bowl over a saucepan of simmering water; beat with a handheld mixer on low speed, then gradually increase the speed to high and beat until soft peaks form, about 5 minutes. Remove the bowl from the pan; continue beating until the meringue is cool and fluffy. Fold in the vanilla, then fold in the melted chocolate until swirled. Spread the meringue on the cake.

RED VELVET LAYER CAKE

SERVES 8 TO 10

ACTIVE: 55 min

TOTAL: 2 hr 10 min

FOR THE CAKE

- 1½ sticks unsalted butter, at room temperature, plus more for the pans
- 3 cups sifted cake flour (sift before measuring)
- 3 tablespoons unsweetened Dutch-process cocoa powder
- 1 teaspoon baking soda
- ½ teaspoon salt
- 1¾ cups granulated sugar
- ⅓ cup vegetable oil
- 3 large eggs, at room temperature
- 1 tablespoon red food coloring
- 2 teaspoons cider vinegar
- 1 teaspoon vanilla extract
- 1 cup buttermilk

FOR THE FROSTING

- 4 8-ounce packages cream cheese, at room temperature
- 2 sticks unsalted butter, at room temperature
- 2 pounds (about 8 cups) confectioners' sugar
- 1 tablespoon lemon juice
- ½ teaspoon vanilla extract
- ⅛ teaspoon salt

We sliced 2 cakes in half horizontally to make this 4-layer cake. To get even layers, stick toothpicks around the sides of each cake as a guide.

1 Make the cake: Preheat the oven to 350°. Butter two 9-inch-round cake pans and line the bottoms with parchment; butter the parchment. Whisk the flour, cocoa powder, baking soda and salt in a bowl.

2 Beat the granulated sugar, 1½ sticks butter and the vegetable oil in a stand mixer fitted with the paddle attachment on medium-high speed until fluffy, about 4 minutes. Beat in the eggs one at a time. Beat in the food coloring, vinegar and vanilla. Reduce the mixer speed to low; add the flour mixture in 3 batches, alternating with the buttermilk, beginning and ending with the flour, until just combined.

3 Divide the batter between the prepared pans. Bake until a toothpick inserted into the center comes out clean, 35 to 40 minutes. Let cool 10 minutes in the pans on racks, then turn the cakes out onto the racks to cool completely. Remove the parchment. Using a long serrated knife, carefully slice each cake in half horizontally to make 2 even layers.

4 Make the frosting: Beat the cream cheese and butter in a stand mixer with the paddle attachment on medium-high speed until fluffy. Add the confectioners' sugar, lemon juice, vanilla and salt; beat until smooth.

5 Put 1 cake layer on a platter; spread 1¼ cups frosting on top. Repeat to make 4 layers, ending with the cake. Cover the top and sides with a thin layer of frosting (this is the crumb coat; it doesn't have to be perfect). Refrigerate 15 minutes, then cover with the remaining frosting.

HUMMINGBIRD CAKE

SERVES 10 TO 12

ACTIVE: 50 min
TOTAL: 2 hr 5 min

FOR THE CAKE

Unsalted butter, for the pans

2¾ cups all-purpose flour, plus
more for dusting

1 cup pecan pieces

3 ripe bananas, chopped

½ cup finely chopped fresh
pineapple

1 teaspoon ground cinnamon

½ teaspoon ground nutmeg

½ teaspoon ground ginger

1¼ teaspoons baking soda

½ teaspoon salt

3 large eggs, at room
temperature

1¾ cups granulated sugar

1 cup vegetable oil

FOR THE FROSTING

2 8-ounce packages cream
cheese, at room temperature

1½ sticks (12 tablespoons)
unsalted butter, cubed, at
room temperature

2 cups confectioners' sugar

1 tablespoon finely grated
lemon zest

1 teaspoon vanilla extract

Some say the name of this classic Southern cake comes from its nectar-like sweetness; others say it's so good, it makes you hum!

1 Make the cake: Preheat the oven to 350°. Butter two 8-inch-round cake pans and line with parchment paper. Butter the parchment and dust with flour.

2 Spread the pecans on a baking sheet and bake until toasted, about 8 minutes. Let cool slightly, then roughly chop. Toss with the bananas, pineapple and ½ cup flour in a small bowl.

3 Whisk the remaining 2¼ cups flour, the cinnamon, nutmeg, ginger, baking soda and salt in a bowl. Beat the eggs and granulated sugar in a separate bowl with a mixer on high speed until thick and light, 5 minutes. Gradually beat in the vegetable oil.

4 Sprinkle the flour mixture over the egg mixture, then gently fold to make a thick batter. Fold in the pecan-fruit mixture, then transfer the batter to the prepared pans. Bake until the cakes are firm and a toothpick inserted into the middle comes out clean, 50 to 55 minutes. Let cool 25 minutes in the pans on a rack, then invert the cakes onto the rack to cool completely. Remove the parchment.

5 Make the frosting: Beat the cream cheese in a large bowl with a mixer until fluffy, then gradually beat in the butter until combined. Sift the confectioners' sugar over the cream cheese mixture and beat until smooth. Add the lemon zest and vanilla and beat until light and fluffy.

6 Place 1 cake layer on a serving plate. Spread about half of the frosting on top, then cover with the other cake layer. Spread the remaining frosting over the top and sides of the cake.

ALMOND LAYER CAKE WITH WHITE CHOCOLATE FROSTING

SERVES 8 TO 10

ACTIVE: 45 min
TOTAL: 1 hr 50 min

FOR THE CAKE

- 1 stick unsalted butter, at room temperature, plus more for the pans
- 2 cups cake flour, plus more for dusting
- 1 tablespoon baking powder
- ½ teaspoon salt
- ½ cup blanched almonds
- 5 large egg whites
- 1 cup whole milk
- 2 teaspoons vanilla extract
- 1½ teaspoons almond extract
- 1½ cups granulated sugar

FOR THE FROSTING

- 8 ounces white chocolate, coarsely chopped
- 2 8-ounce packages cream cheese, at room temperature
- 1½ sticks (12 tablespoons) unsalted butter, at room temperature
- 1 cup confectioners' sugar
- 2 teaspoons vanilla extract
- White nonpareils or sprinkles, for topping

These layers can be made in advance: Just place the cooled cakes in plastic wrap and freeze for up to 2 weeks; unwrap and thaw at room temperature before frosting.

1 Make the cake: Preheat the oven to 350°. Lightly butter two 9-inch-round cake pans and line the bottoms with parchment paper; butter the parchment and dust with flour, tapping out the excess. Pulse 2 cups flour, the baking powder, salt and almonds in a food processor until the nuts are ground into a powder, 2 to 3 minutes. Whisk the egg whites, milk, and vanilla and almond extracts in a medium bowl until combined.

2 Beat 1 stick butter and the granulated sugar in a large bowl with a mixer on medium speed until light and fluffy, about 3 minutes. Reduce the mixer speed to low; beat in the flour mixture in 3 additions, alternating with the milk mixture, beginning and ending with the flour, until just combined.

3 Divide the batter between the prepared pans and smooth the tops. Bake until a toothpick inserted into the centers comes out clean, 25 to 30 minutes. Transfer to racks and let cool in the pans.

4 Make the frosting: Microwave the white chocolate in a microwave-safe bowl in 20-second intervals, stirring, until melted; set aside. Beat the cream cheese, butter, confectioners' sugar and vanilla in a large bowl with a mixer on medium speed until creamy, about 4 minutes. Gently fold in the melted white chocolate with a rubber spatula.

5 Assemble the cake: Loosen the edges of the cakes with a knife, then invert 1 layer onto a platter and peel off the parchment. Spread 1 to 1½ cups frosting on top. Remove the other layer from the pan, peel off the parchment and carefully place on top of the first layer. Cover the top and sides of the cake with a thin layer of frosting (this is the crumb coat; it doesn't have to be perfect). Chill 15 minutes, then cover with the remaining frosting and decorate with nonpareils.

HAZELNUT DACQUOISE

SERVES 10 TO 12

ACTIVE: 1 hr

TOTAL: 4 hr 30 min (plus chilling)

1⅓ cups blanched hazelnuts

1½ cups plus ⅓ cup sugar

1 tablespoon kosher potato starch

6 large egg whites

¼ teaspoon salt

¼ cup whole milk

5 cups heavy cream

8 ounces bittersweet chocolate, coarsely chopped, plus shaved chocolate for topping

1 tablespoon instant espresso powder

Dacquoise is a French dessert made of meringue layers and a cream filling. Prepare it a day ahead so the meringue softens.

1 Position racks in the upper and lower thirds of the oven; preheat to 325°. Toast the hazelnuts on a baking sheet, 12 to 15 minutes; let cool. Combine 1 cup each hazelnuts and sugar and the potato starch in a food processor and pulse until very finely ground; place in a large bowl.

2 Reduce the oven temperature to 275°. Line 2 baking sheets with parchment. Draw three 7-inch circles on the parchment with a pencil (2 on 1 piece and 1 on the other); flip the parchment so the markings face down. Put the egg whites, ½ cup sugar and the salt in a heatproof bowl set over a saucepan of simmering water (don't let the bowl touch the water). Whisk until the sugar is dissolved and the mixture is warm. Remove the bowl from the saucepan; beat with a mixer on medium-high speed until stiff and shiny but not dry, about 2 minutes.

3 Fold the milk and one-quarter of the egg white mixture into the nut mixture with a rubber spatula until smooth; fold in the remaining egg whites until just combined. Divide the batter among the 3 circles on the parchment and spread evenly. Bake 1 hour, 30 minutes, then switch the position of the pans and continue baking until the layers are dry, golden and peel easily off the parchment, 1 to 2 more hours. Let cool slightly on the baking sheets; peel off the parchment and cool completely on racks.

4 Make the ganache: Microwave 1 cup cream in a microwave-safe bowl until hot, 2 minutes. Whisk in the chocolate and espresso powder until smooth. Let cool; cover and refrigerate until thick and spreadable, at least 30 minutes. Beat the remaining 4 cups cream and ⅓ cup sugar with a mixer on medium speed until it barely holds soft peaks, 1 to 2 minutes. Finish beating with a whisk just until soft peaks form.

5 Put 2 meringue layers on a baking sheet; spread half of the ganache on each. (If the ganache is too firm, microwave in 20-second intervals.) Refrigerate the layers until set, 15 minutes. Place one of the ganache-topped meringues on a platter. Spread with 1 cup whipped cream. Stack the other ganache-topped meringue on top; spread with another layer of whipped cream. Top with the last meringue, then cover the top and side of the cake with the remaining whipped cream. Chop the remaining toasted hazelnuts and sprinkle on the cake along with the shaved chocolate. Refrigerate at least 6 hours or overnight before serving.

③ TWISTS ON VANILLA CAKE

MAKES TWO 9-INCH LAYERS

ACTIVE: 20 min

TOTAL: 1 hr 20 min

- 2 sticks unsalted butter, at room temperature, plus more for the pans
- 3 cups all-purpose flour, plus more for the pans
- 1 tablespoon baking powder
- ½ teaspoon salt
- 1½ cups sugar
- 4 large eggs, at room temperature
- 1 tablespoon vanilla extract
- ¾ cup heavy cream

This is a perfect base for a birthday cake: You can customize the fillings and frostings with anyone's favorite flavors.

1 Preheat the oven to 350°. Butter two 9-inch-round cake pans and line the bottoms with parchment paper; butter the parchment and dust the pans with flour, tapping out the excess.

2 Whisk 3 cups flour, the baking powder and salt in a bowl until combined. Beat 2 sticks butter and the sugar in a large bowl with a mixer on medium-high speed until light and fluffy, about 3 minutes. Reduce the mixer speed to medium; beat in the eggs, one at a time, scraping down the bowl as needed. Beat in the vanilla. (The mixture may look separated at this point.)

3 Mix ½ cup water with the cream in a liquid measuring cup or bowl. Beat the flour mixture into the butter mixture in 3 batches, alternating with the cream mixture in 2 batches, beginning and ending with flour, until just smooth.

4 Divide the batter between the prepared pans. Bake until the cakes are lightly golden on top and the centers spring back when pressed, 25 to 30 minutes. Transfer to racks and let cool 10 minutes, then run a knife around the edges of the pans and turn the cakes out onto the racks to cool completely. Remove the parchment. Trim the tops of the cakes with a long serrated knife to make them level, if desired.

LEMON MERINGUE CAKE

Spread lemon curd between 2 cake layers. For the meringue, whisk 4 egg whites and 1 cup sugar in a heatproof bowl set over a saucepan of simmering water until the sugar dissolves, 3 to 4 minutes. Remove the bowl, then beat in a pinch of cream of tartar and ½ teaspoon vanilla with a mixer on medium-high speed until stiff, glossy peaks form, 6 to 8 minutes. Cover the top and sides of the cake with the meringue, then brown using a kitchen torch.

COOKIES-AND-CREAM CAKE

Melt 6 ounces chopped white chocolate in the microwave in 30-second intervals, stirring; let cool slightly. Beat 3 sticks softened butter, 1 teaspoon vanilla and a pinch of salt with a mixer on medium-high speed, 1 minute. Beat in the melted white chocolate. Gradually beat in 3 cups confectioners' sugar. Spread some frosting on 1 cake layer, sprinkle with crushed chocolate sandwich cookies. Top with the other layer. Cover the cake with the remaining frosting and more cookies.

PINEAPPLE-COCONUT CAKE

Poke holes all over the tops of both layers using a toothpick; brush with ¼ cup pineapple juice. Bring 1¼ cups chopped dried pineapple, ½ cup pineapple juice, ¼ cup cream of coconut and ½ cup water to a simmer. Cook over medium heat, stirring occasionally, until syrupy, 20 minutes. Let cool, then mash with a fork. Spread between the cake layers. Make the frosting: Beat 2½ sticks softened butter and a pinch of salt with a mixer until fluffy. Gradually beat in 2¼ cups confectioners' sugar. Add ¼ cup cream of coconut and beat until thick. Frost the cake; top with toasted coconut and dried pineapple.

THREE-LAYER CARROT CAKE

SERVES 10 TO 12

ACTIVE: 1 hr
TOTAL: 1 hr 50 min (plus chilling)

FOR THE CAKE

¾ cup vegetable oil, plus more for the pans

1 cup pecan halves

2 cups all-purpose flour

2 teaspoons baking powder

1½ teaspoons baking soda

2 teaspoons ground cinnamon

1 teaspoon ground ginger

1 teaspoon salt

¾ cup granulated sugar

1 teaspoon finely grated lemon zest

4 large eggs

½ cup plus 3 tablespoons orange marmalade, plus more for topping

3 cups shredded carrots

FOR THE FROSTING

3 8-ounce packages cream cheese, at room temperature

1½ sticks unsalted butter, at room temperature

3 cups confectioners' sugar

1 tablespoon lemon juice

1 tablespoon vanilla extract

Pinch of salt

Don't let the marmalade in this recipe scare anyone off: The bitterness is offset by the sweet cake and frosting.

1 Make the cake: Position racks in the upper and lower thirds of the oven and preheat to 350°. Brush three 9-inch-round cake pans with vegetable oil and line the bottoms with parchment paper. Spread the pecans on a baking sheet and bake until toasted, about 10 minutes. Let cool, then pulse in a food processor until very finely chopped.

2 Combine the pecans, flour, baking powder, baking soda, cinnamon, ginger, salt and granulated sugar in a large bowl. In another bowl, whisk the vegetable oil, lemon zest, eggs and ½ cup marmalade. Stir in the carrots, then fold the carrot mixture into the flour mixture until just combined. Divide among the prepared pans and spread evenly (it won't look like a lot of batter, but the cakes will rise in the oven). Put 2 pans on the upper oven rack and the third pan on the lower rack. Bake until the cakes bounce back when touched and a toothpick comes out clean, 20 to 25 minutes, switching the position of the pans halfway through. Transfer the pans to racks until cool enough to handle, then invert the cakes onto the racks to cool completely. Remove the parchment.

3 Make the frosting: Beat the cream cheese and butter in a bowl with a mixer until smooth, scraping down the bowl as needed. Beat in the confectioners' sugar, lemon juice, vanilla and salt until smooth.

4 Put 1 of the cake layers on a platter. Spread with 1 tablespoon of the remaining marmalade, then spread about ¾ cup frosting over the marmalade. Top with another cake layer, marmalade and frosting. Spread the final cake layer with a thin layer of frosting (this is the crumb coat; it doesn't have to be perfect). Refrigerate 1 hour, then cover with the remaining frosting. Swirl some marmalade into the top of the cake. Refrigerate until ready to serve.

PEPPERMINT LAYER CAKE WITH CANDY CANE FROSTING

SERVES 8 TO 10

ACTIVE: 1 hr 15 min

TOTAL: 3 hr

FOR THE CAKE

- 1½ sticks unsalted butter, at room temperature, plus more for the pans
- 2 cups sifted cake flour (sift before measuring), plus more for dusting
- 1½ teaspoons baking powder
- ¾ teaspoon salt
- ¾ cup whole milk, at room temperature
- 1 teaspoon vanilla extract
- ½ teaspoon peppermint extract
- 1½ cups sugar
- 3 large egg whites, at room temperature

FOR THE FROSTING

- 1½ cups sugar
- ½ cup light corn syrup
- 6 large egg whites
  Pinch of salt
- ½ teaspoon vanilla extract
- ½ teaspoon peppermint extract
- ¼ cup crushed candy canes, plus more for topping

To get light, airy cakes, be sure to sift the flour first, then scoop it into your measuring cup and level it with a knife.

1 Make the cake: Position racks in the middle and lower thirds of the oven and preheat to 350°. Lightly butter three 8-inch-round cake pans and line the bottoms with parchment; butter the parchment and dust with flour. Sift the flour, baking powder and salt into a medium bowl. Combine the milk and the vanilla and peppermint extracts in a bowl.

2 Beat the butter with a mixer on medium speed until smooth, about 1 minute. Gradually beat in 1 cup sugar, then increase the mixer speed to high and continue beating until light and fluffy, about 5 minutes. Reduce the mixer speed to low and add the flour mixture in 3 additions, alternating with the milk mixture, beginning and ending with the flour mixture, until just combined. Scrape down the bowl, then increase the mixer speed to medium and beat until smooth, 5 more minutes.

3 In a large bowl, using clean beaters, beat the egg whites on high speed until foamy. Gradually add the remaining ½ cup sugar and beat until stiff, shiny peaks form. Using a rubber spatula, gently fold the whites into the batter in 3 additions. Divide the batter among the pans. Bake, switching the position of the pans halfway through, until a toothpick inserted in the center comes out clean, about 20 minutes. Let the cakes cool 10 minutes in the pans, then run a knife around the edges and invert onto racks to cool completely. Peel off the parchment.

4 Make the frosting: Fill a saucepan with 1 inch of water and bring to a simmer over medium-high heat. Whisk the sugar, corn syrup, egg whites, 2 tablespoons water and the salt in a heatproof bowl set over the saucepan until the mixture registers 165° on a candy thermometer, about 8 minutes. (Don't let the bowl touch the water.) Remove the bowl from the pan and beat with a mixer on medium speed until soft peaks form, about 5 minutes. Increase the mixer speed to high and beat until fluffy, 4 more minutes. Beat in the vanilla and peppermint extracts.

5 Place 1 cake layer on a platter; spread with 1 cup frosting and sprinkle with some crushed candy canes. Repeat with the remaining layers, then cover the cake with the remaining frosting and crushed candy canes.

SALTED CARAMEL–ORANGE UPSIDE-DOWN CAKE

SERVES 8 TO 10

ACTIVE: 40 min
TOTAL: 1 hr 55 min

FOR THE CARAMEL

⅔ cup sugar

¼ teaspoon kosher salt

1 tablespoon salted butter

5 oranges

FOR THE CAKE

½ cup sliced almonds

1¼ cups all-purpose flour

¾ teaspoon baking powder

¾ teaspoon baking soda

¼ teaspoon kosher salt

1 stick salted butter, at room temperature

⅔ cup sugar

2 large eggs

1 teaspoon grated orange zest

½ cup sour cream

Sea salt, for sprinkling

Learn how to "supreme" oranges in this recipe: The term just means you're removing the orange peel, pith and membranes, so you end up with pretty segments.

1 Make the caramel: Combine the sugar, ⅓ cup water and the kosher salt in a medium saucepan over medium heat, stirring just until the sugar dissolves. Cook, gently swirling the pan occasionally but not stirring, until amber, 8 to 10 minutes. Brush any sugar crystals off the side of the pan with a wet pastry brush. Remove from the heat and carefully whisk in the butter (the mixture will bubble). Pour into a 9-inch-round cake pan, tilting the pan to coat the bottom; set aside.

2 Slice off the top and bottom of the oranges. Place the oranges cut-side down and cut off the peel and white pith with a chef's knife, following the curve of the fruit. Cut along both sides of each membrane to remove the segments. Set the segments aside, discarding any seeds.

3 Make the cake: Preheat the oven to 350°. Spread the almonds on a baking sheet and bake until golden brown, 8 to 10 minutes. Let cool, then transfer to a food processor and pulse until finely ground. Transfer to a medium bowl; add the flour, baking powder, baking soda and kosher salt and whisk to combine.

4 Beat the butter and sugar in a large bowl with a mixer on medium-high speed until fluffy, about 5 minutes. Beat in the eggs one at a time, scraping down the bowl as needed. Beat in the orange zest. Reduce the mixer speed to low; beat in the flour mixture in 3 batches, alternating with the sour cream, beginning and ending with flour, until just smooth.

5 Arrange the orange segments in the cake pan in concentric circles. Add the batter and smooth the top. Bake until golden brown and a toothpick inserted into the center comes out clean, 40 to 45 minutes. (Tent with foil if the top gets too dark.) Transfer to a rack and let cool slightly, then run a knife around the edge of the cake and invert onto a platter. Let cool completely. Sprinkle with sea salt.

RED VELVET CHEESECAKE

SERVES 10

ACTIVE: 35 min

TOTAL: 2 hr 20 min (plus chilling)

FOR THE CRUST

- 1½ cups finely crushed chocolate wafer cookies (about 28 cookies)
- 5 tablespoons unsalted butter, melted
- ⅓ cup sugar
- Pinch of salt

FOR THE FILLING

- 4 8-ounce packages cream cheese, at room temperature
- 1¼ cups sugar
- 1 tablespoon fresh lemon juice
- 1 teaspoon vanilla extract
- 2 tablespoons all-purpose flour
- 4 large eggs
- 1 tablespoon unsweetened cocoa powder
- 1 teaspoon red food coloring

To get clean slices when you're cutting cheesecake, dip your knife in hot water, wipe dry, then repeat between each cut.

1 Make the crust: Preheat the oven to 350°. Mix the cookie crumbs, melted butter, sugar and salt in a bowl. Press into the bottom and 1 inch up the sides of a 9-inch springform pan. Put the pan on a baking sheet and bake until set, about 10 minutes. Let cool completely.

2 Make the filling: Reduce the oven temperature to 325°. Beat the cream cheese, sugar, lemon juice and vanilla in a stand mixer fitted with the paddle attachment until smooth, 4 to 5 minutes. Add the flour, then beat in the eggs one at a time. Transfer 2 cups batter to a bowl; stir in the cocoa powder and food coloring. Pour the red batter into the crust, then pour the white batter on top. Using a spoon, pull some of the red batter up from the bottom of the cake and swirl. Bake until the edges are set but the center is still wobbly, about 1 hour, 20 minutes.

3 Turn off the oven but keep the cake inside to cool, 20 minutes. Run a knife around the edge of the pan (don't remove the side), then transfer to a rack to cool. Refrigerate at least 4 hours before removing the springform ring and slicing.

ROCKY ROAD CHEESECAKE

SERVES 8

ACTIVE: 50 min

TOTAL: 3 hr 10 min (plus chilling)

Cooking spray

6 chocolate wafer cookies

20 ounces cream cheese (2½ eight-ounce packages), at room temperature

1¼ cups sugar

3 large eggs, at room temperature

1 cup heavy cream

2 teaspoons vanilla extract

1½ ounces semisweet chocolate, finely chopped

2 tablespoons unsweetened cocoa powder

2 meringue cookies, coarsely crushed

2 tablespoons salted peanuts, chopped

Creating the bull's-eye effect in this cake is much easier than it looks: Just alternate pouring the vanilla and chocolate batters into the center of the pan to create two-toned rings.

1 Fill a large roasting pan about one-third of the way with water and carefully place on the middle oven rack. Preheat the oven to 325°. Wrap the outside of an 8-inch springform pan with foil. Coat the inside of the pan with cooking spray.

2 Finely crush 3 chocolate cookies and sprinkle the crumbs in the bottom of the springform pan; tap out the excess. Beat the cream cheese in a large bowl with a mixer on medium-high speed until light and fluffy, about 3 minutes. Add the sugar, eggs, ¾ cup cream and the vanilla. Reduce the mixer speed to medium and beat until the sugar is dissolved and the mixture is creamy, scraping down the bowl as needed. (Do not overbeat; if there are still lumps, whisk the batter by hand to smooth them out.)

3 Put the chocolate and the remaining ¼ cup cream in a microwave-safe bowl and microwave until the chocolate melts, about 45 seconds. Stir in the cocoa powder until smooth.

4 Divide the batter between 2 large liquid measuring cups or bowls (about 2½ cups batter in each). Stir the melted chocolate mixture into one of the batters. Pour about half of the vanilla batter into the springform pan, then slowly pour half of the chocolate batter into the center of the vanilla, letting it spread. Pour the remaining vanilla batter into the center of the chocolate batter, letting it spread; pour the remaining chocolate batter into the middle.

5 Carefully transfer the cheesecake to the pan of hot water and bake until the edges are set but the center still jiggles slightly, 1 hour, 30 minutes to 1 hour, 45 minutes. Turn off the oven and keep the cake in the oven with the door ajar, 30 minutes. Remove the cake from the water bath and transfer to a rack. Run a knife around the edges of the cake to loosen and let cool completely, then refrigerate overnight.

6 Remove the springform ring. Crush the remaining 3 chocolate cookies and toss in a bowl with the crushed meringues and chopped peanuts. Press into the sides of the cake.

WHITE CHOCOLATE-CRANBERRY CHEESECAKE

SERVES 8 TO 10

ACTIVE: 1 hr
TOTAL: 3 hr 40 min (plus chilling)

FOR THE CRUST

- 18 whole graham crackers
- 2 tablespoons sugar
- Pinch of ground nutmeg
- Pinch of salt
- 5 tablespoons unsalted butter, melted and cooled

FOR THE FILLING

- 4 ounces white chocolate, chopped, plus shaved chocolate for topping
- 4 8-ounce packages cream cheese, at room temperature
- 1 cup sour cream
- 1 cup plus 2 tablespoons sugar
- 4 large eggs
- 2 tablespoons cornstarch
- 1 teaspoon vanilla extract
- Pinch of salt

FOR THE TOPPING

- 1 1-pound bag cranberries
- 1 cup sugar
- 1 teaspoon grated orange zest
- 2 tablespoons orange juice

Use gentle heat when you're melting white chocolate. It melts at a lower temperature than semisweet and scorches easily.

1 Make the crust: Set racks in the lower third and middle of the oven; preheat to 350°. Finely crush the graham crackers, then mix with the sugar, nutmeg and salt in a bowl. Add the melted butter and mix with your hands until combined. Press into the bottom and 1 inch up the sides of a 9-inch springform pan. Freeze until ready to fill.

2 Make the filling: Bring 1 inch of water to a boil in a small pot; remove from the heat. Put the white chocolate in a heatproof bowl and set over the pot (do not let the bowl touch the water); stir until melted, about 4 minutes. Remove the bowl from the pot and set aside. Beat the cream cheese, sour cream and sugar in a large bowl with a mixer on medium-high speed until light and fluffy, about 7 minutes. Beat in the eggs, one at a time, then add the cornstarch and beat 2 minutes. Beat in the melted white chocolate, vanilla and salt until combined.

3 Fill a roasting pan halfway with water and set on the lower oven rack. Pour the filling into the crust and set on the middle oven rack. Bake until the edge is set but the center jiggles slightly, 1 hour, 10 minutes. Turn off the oven and leave the cheesecake inside for 30 minutes. Transfer to a rack to cool completely, then cover and refrigerate 8 hours or overnight.

4 Make the topping: Spread the cranberries on a rimmed baking sheet, sprinkle with ⅓ cup sugar and set aside until they release some of their juices, about 1 hour. Meanwhile, combine the remaining ⅔ cup sugar, the orange zest and juice, and ¾ cup water in a medium saucepan. Bring to a boil, stirring, then reduce the heat to medium low and simmer until thick enough to coat the back of a spoon, about 10 minutes. Drain the cranberries and add them to the saucepan. Cook, stirring, until they begin to burst, about 7 minutes. Transfer to a bowl and refrigerate.

5 Before serving, run a hot knife around the edge of the cheesecake, then remove the springform ring. Top with the chilled cranberry mixture and shaved white chocolate.

CHEESECAKE WITH LEMON–GINGER CURD

SERVES 8

ACTIVE: 1 hr

TOTAL: 2 hr 50 min (plus chilling)

FOR THE CRUST

8 whole graham crackers, broken into pieces

1½ cups lightly crushed butter cookies

5 tablespoons unsalted butter, melted

FOR THE FILLING

3 8-ounce packages cream cheese, at room temperature

1 cup sugar

3 large eggs

2 tablespoons fresh Meyer lemon juice

1½ teaspoons vanilla extract

FOR THE LEMON CURD

1 4-inch piece ginger, peeled

3 large eggs

½ cup sugar

1 tablespoon heavy cream

½ cup fresh Meyer lemon juice (about 4 lemons)

2 tablespoons cold unsalted butter, cut into small pieces

We used Meyer lemons for this dessert, which are slightly sweeter than regular ones. They're in season in winter and early spring; if you can't get them, just use equal parts lemon juice and orange juice.

1 Make the crust: Preheat the oven to 350°. Pulse the graham crackers and butter cookies in a food processor until finely ground; drizzle in the melted butter and pulse to combine. Press the crumb mixture into the bottom and about 1 inch up the sides of a 9-inch springform pan. Bake until golden, about 10 minutes, then transfer to a rack and let cool completely. Reduce the oven temperature to 300°.

2 Make the filling: Beat the cream cheese and sugar in a large bowl with a mixer on medium-high speed until smooth and slightly fluffy, about 3 minutes. Beat in the eggs, one at a time, then beat in the lemon juice and vanilla. Pour the batter into the crust. Transfer to the oven and bake until the edges are set but the center still jiggles slightly, 1 hour to 1 hour, 10 minutes. Turn off the oven and keep the cheesecake in the oven with the door ajar, 20 minutes. Remove from the oven and run a knife around the edge of the cake to loosen. Transfer to a rack; let cool completely, then refrigerate until set, at least 4 hours or overnight.

3 Make the lemon curd: Finely grate the ginger; put in a fine-mesh sieve set over a bowl and press with a rubber spatula to extract the juice.

4 Whisk the eggs, sugar and cream in a small nonreactive saucepan until combined. Add the lemon juice and ginger juice and cook over medium heat, whisking constantly, until thick and bubbly, about 6 minutes. Remove from the heat and whisk in the butter until melted. Strain the curd through a fine-mesh sieve set over a bowl, pressing it through with a rubber spatula; let cool. Refrigerate until ready to use.

5 Spread the curd over the cheesecake and refrigerate until set, about 30 minutes. Remove the springform ring and slice.

Fun Project!
COLOR YOUR FROSTING

You can create frosting in amazing colors with a standard box of food coloring. To make one of the colors on this chart, dye 1 cup of store-bought white frosting with the number of drops of red (r), blue (b), yellow (y) or green (g) food coloring listed here. Don't be alarmed: 100 drops of food coloring is only about 1 teaspoon!

RASPBERRY SORBET
111r

COSMOPOLITAN
45r, 5y

CHERRY BLOSSOM
11r, 3y

CIRCUS PEANUT
6r, 8y

CREAMSICLE
11r, 9y

PAPAYA
45r, 80y

BANANA PUDDING
20y

LEMON BAR
49y

PIÑA COLADA
3y

HONEYDEW
2g, 5y

SOUR APPLE
5b, 45y

KEY LIME
30g, 25y

MOJITO
54b, 27y

WATERMELON
46b, 78g

BLUE RASPBERRY
108b, 30g

WILD BLUEBERRY
58b

JORDAN ALMOND
12b

ICE
4b

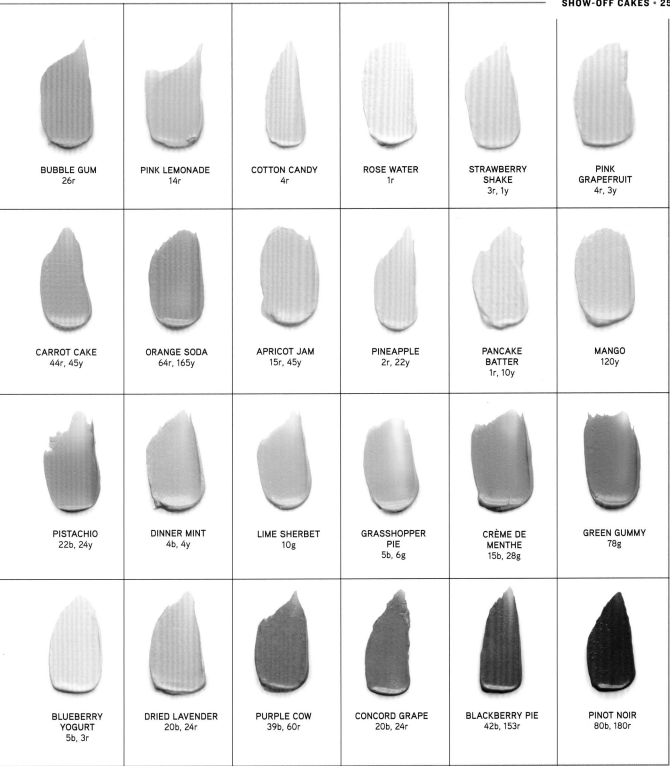

| BUBBLE GUM | PINK LEMONADE | COTTON CANDY | ROSE WATER | STRAWBERRY SHAKE | PINK GRAPEFRUIT |
| 26r | 14r | 4r | 1r | 3r, 1y | 4r, 3y |

| CARROT CAKE | ORANGE SODA | APRICOT JAM | PINEAPPLE | PANCAKE BATTER | MANGO |
| 44r, 45y | 64r, 165y | 15r, 45y | 2r, 22y | 1r, 10y | 120y |

| PISTACHIO | DINNER MINT | LIME SHERBET | GRASSHOPPER PIE | CRÈME DE MENTHE | GREEN GUMMY |
| 22b, 24y | 4b, 4y | 10g | 5b, 6g | 15b, 28g | 78g |

| BLUEBERRY YOGURT | DRIED LAVENDER | PURPLE COW | CONCORD GRAPE | BLACKBERRY PIE | PINOT NOIR |
| 5b, 3r | 20b, 24r | 39b, 60r | 20b, 24r | 42b, 153r | 80b, 180r |

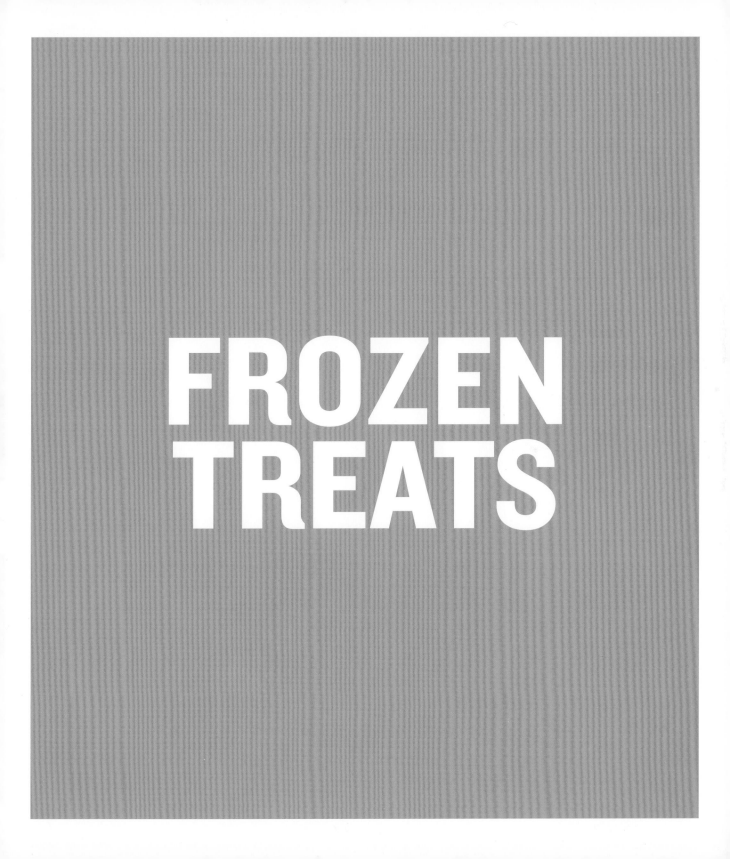

FROZEN
TREATS

PEACH COBBLER ICE CREAM CAKE

SERVES 12

ACTIVE: 40 min

TOTAL: 7 hr

1½ cups granulated sugar

   Juice of 1 lemon

4 peaches, peeled and cut into ¾-inch pieces

1 sleeve graham crackers (9 whole crackers)

½ cup chopped pecans

4 tablespoons unsalted butter, melted

4 pints vanilla ice cream

   Cooking spray

2 10-to-12-ounce pound cakes

1½ cups cold heavy cream

3 tablespoons confectioners' sugar

2 teaspoons vanilla extract

Whipped cream is the perfect topping for ice cream cakes: It holds up better in the freezer than standard frosting.

1 Stir 1¼ cups granulated sugar, the lemon juice and peaches in a pot; let sit 15 minutes. Bring to a simmer, then reduce the heat to low and cook until the peaches are tender, about 15 minutes. Remove ¾ cup peaches with a slotted spoon and set aside in the refrigerator for topping. Puree the remaining peaches and cooking liquid in a blender; transfer to a bowl and freeze until very thick, about 1 hour.

2 Preheat the oven to 350°; line a baking sheet with foil. Coarsely crush the graham crackers and toss with the remaining ¼ cup granulated sugar, the pecans and butter on the prepared baking sheet; spread into a thin layer. Bake 7 minutes, then stir and continue baking until golden brown, 6 to 10 more minutes. Let cool, then crumble and set aside.

3 Assemble the cake: Let 2 pints ice cream soften at room temperature until spreadable, about 10 minutes. Coat a 9-inch springform pan with cooking spray and line the bottom and sides with plastic wrap, leaving a 2-inch overhang. Spread the softened ice cream in the prepared pan with an offset spatula, then top evenly with the peach puree. Freeze until the puree is firm, about 45 minutes.

4 Let the remaining 2 pints ice cream soften, 10 minutes, then spread over the peach puree. Sprinkle with 1 cup of the pecan mixture, then press it into the ice cream. Cut the pound cakes lengthwise into 1½-inch-thick slices; place the slices in a single layer on top of the ice cream, trimming as needed. Cover with plastic wrap and freeze until firm, at least 6 hours or overnight.

5 Beat the heavy cream, confectioners' sugar and vanilla in a bowl with a mixer on medium speed until soft peaks form. Uncover the cake, then invert onto a plate; remove the springform ring and the remaining plastic wrap. Cover the top and sides with the whipped cream. Top with the reserved peach pieces and remaining pecan mixture. Freeze until firm, about 1 hour.

NEAPOLITAN ICE CREAM CAKE

SERVES 8

ACTIVE: 25 min

TOTAL: 4 hr 25 min

- 10 3.5-ounce rectangular vanilla ice cream sandwiches
- 1 pint strawberry ice cream, slightly softened
- 1 pint mint chip or pistachio ice cream, slightly softened
- ½ cup finely crushed chocolate wafer cookies (about 12 cookies)
- ½ cup chocolate shell ice cream topping

No one will guess the secret to this easy cake: basic ice cream sandwiches!

1 Line a 9-by-5-inch loaf pan with heavy-duty foil, leaving an overhang on all sides. Arrange 5 ice cream sandwiches snugly in the bottom of the pan. Spread the strawberry ice cream on top in an even layer. Press the remaining 5 ice cream sandwiches on top, then spread the mint chip ice cream evenly over the sandwiches. Top with an even layer of crushed cookies, pressing gently.

2 Cover the cake with plastic wrap and freeze until set, about 4 hours. Uncover, then lift the foil to remove the cake from the pan. Invert onto a platter, remove the foil and spread with chocolate shell topping. Serve immediately or cover and freeze for up to 2 days.

TOASTED MARSHMALLOW ICE CREAM CAKE

SERVES 8

ACTIVE: 20 min

TOTAL: 2 hr 30 min

- ¾ cup graham cracker crumbs (from about 6 whole crackers)
- ¾ cup pecans, finely ground
- 2 tablespoons sugar
- 3 tablespoons unsalted butter, melted
- ¼ cup chocolate syrup
- 2 quarts vanilla ice cream, slightly softened
- 2 cups mini marshmallows

When you're making an ice cream cake, the ice cream should be just soft enough to spread (not melted). Leave the carton at room temperature for 10 to 15 minutes before you start.

1 Stir the graham cracker crumbs, pecans, sugar and butter in a bowl until combined. Press the crumb mixture into the bottom of a 9-inch springform pan. Drizzle with the chocolate syrup and freeze until firm, about 15 minutes.

2 Spread the vanilla ice cream over the chocolate-drizzled crust in a smooth, even layer, packing the ice cream into the pan. Freeze until firm, about 2 hours.

3 Remove the cake from the freezer and top with the marshmallows. Toast the topping with a kitchen torch or broil about 4 inches away from the heat until the marshmallows are puffed and evenly browned, rotating the pan as needed.

4 Return the cake to the freezer for 15 minutes. Run a knife around the edges of the cake before removing the side of the pan. Serve immediately or freeze for up to 2 days.

ICE CREAM CRUNCH CAKE

SERVES 10 TO 12

ACTIVE: 1 hr
TOTAL: 5 hr 50 min

2 1½-quart containers vanilla ice cream

1 9-ounce package chocolate wafer cookies

1 7-to-8-ounce bottle chocolate shell ice cream topping

1 1½-quart container chocolate ice cream

5 cups whipped cream

Rainbow sprinkles, for decorating

This classic-looking ice cream cake is perfect for a birthday party: You can customize it with a child's favorite flavors.

1 Put a 9-inch springform pan in the freezer for 15 minutes. Meanwhile, let 1 container vanilla ice cream soften at room temperature.

2 Remove the pan from the freezer. Spread a ½-inch-thick layer of softened vanilla ice cream on the bottom and up the sides of the pan. (If the ice cream gets too soft, return it to the freezer.) Freeze until firm, about 45 minutes.

3 Meanwhile, pulse the chocolate cookies in a food processor to break into large crumbs. Add the chocolate shell topping and pulse until the crumbs are moist, about 5 pulses; set aside.

4 Let the chocolate ice cream soften at room temperature, about 15 minutes. Spread over the vanilla layer, firmly packing the ice cream into the pan. Spread the chocolate crumb mixture over the chocolate ice cream. Freeze until set, about 1 hour.

5 Remove the remaining container of vanilla ice cream from the freezer 15 minutes before assembling the final layer. Spread the ice cream over the crumb layer, packing it tightly, then smooth the top with an offset spatula. Freeze until firm, about 2 hours.

6 To unmold, wipe the outside of the pan with a hot cloth, then run a hot knife around the inside; remove the springform ring. If the ice cream cake is too soft, refreeze 20 minutes.

7 Spread 3 cups whipped cream over the top and sides of the cake. Freeze until set, about 20 minutes. Put the remaining 2 cups whipped cream in a pastry bag fitted with a star tip; pipe along the top and bottom edges of the cake and decorate with sprinkles. Return to the freezer; remove 15 minutes before serving and slice with a hot knife.

LEMON-RASPBERRY SORBET CAKE

SERVES 8 TO 10

ACTIVE: 30 min

TOTAL: 2 hr 25 min

- 3 tablespoons unsalted butter, melted, plus softened butter for the pan
- ¾ cup finely crushed chocolate wafer cookies (about 15 cookies)
- 1 tablespoon sugar
- 3 pints lemon sorbet, slightly softened
- 3 pints raspberry sorbet, slightly softened
- 6 ounces bittersweet chocolate, finely chopped
- ⅓ cup heavy cream

You don't need a special pan to make this extra-tall cake: Just line a springform pan with a wide strip of parchment paper to build up the sides.

1 Cut a 24-by-6-inch strip of parchment paper. Butter the sides of an 8-inch springform pan, then line the sides with the parchment; the paper will extend above the rim of the pan so you can build a tall cake.

2 Mix the crushed cookies, sugar and melted butter in a bowl until combined. Press the mixture into the bottom and about ¼ inch up the sides of the prepared pan. Freeze until firm, about 15 minutes.

3 Scoop the lemon sorbet over the crust in small batches, packing it in with an offset spatula; smooth the top. Freeze until firm, about 45 minutes. Repeat with the raspberry sorbet and freeze until firm, about 45 more minutes.

4 Place the chocolate in a heatproof bowl. Heat the cream in a small saucepan or in the microwave until barely simmering; pour the hot cream over the chocolate and let stand 1 minute, then stir until smooth. Remove the springform ring and the parchment. Spread the chocolate mixture over the top of the cake and freeze until set, about 10 minutes. Serve immediately or cover and freeze for up to 2 days.

SALTED CARAMEL ICE CREAM CONE CAKE

SERVES 6 TO 8

ACTIVE: 30 min

TOTAL: 6 hr 30 min

    Unsalted butter, for the pan

14 pizzelle (thin Italian waffle cookies) or thin butter cookies

¾ cup chocolate fudge sauce

1 quart vanilla-caramel swirl ice cream, slightly softened

1 quart chocolate ice cream, slightly softened

½ cup dulce de leche or caramel sauce

½ teaspoon flaky sea salt

5 sugar cones

¼ cup toffee bits

Salt is surprisingly delicious on ice cream (try a pinch on a scoop if you're skeptical). We used flaky Maldon sea salt on this fun cake.

1 Cut a 24-by-6-inch strip of parchment paper. Butter the sides of an 8-inch springform pan, then line the sides with the parchment; the paper will extend above the rim of the pan so you can build a tall cake.

2 Cover the bottom of the pan with half of the cookies, breaking them into smaller pieces as needed to cover the surface. Spread ¼ cup fudge sauce over the cookies.

3 Pack about half of the vanilla-caramel and chocolate ice cream into the pan, alternating scoops of each flavor, until the bottom is covered. Drizzle with ¼ cup dulce de leche and sprinkle with ¼ teaspoon sea salt. Top with the remaining cookies, pressing gently to pack in the ice cream and create an even surface.

4 Spread ¼ cup fudge sauce over the cookies. Top with scoops of the remaining vanilla-caramel and chocolate ice creams. Drizzle with the remaining ¼ cup each dulce de leche and fudge sauce and sprinkle with the remaining ¼ teaspoon sea salt. Arrange the ice cream cones, point-side up, on top. Freeze until firm, at least 6 hours or overnight.

5 Remove the sides of the springform pan and the parchment. Press the toffee bits into the sides of the cake. Serve immediately or freeze for up to 2 days.

BAKED ALASKA

SERVES 12

ACTIVE: 45 min
TOTAL: 6 hr 25 min

FOR THE ICE CREAM CAKE

Vegetable oil, for brushing

1 pint raspberry, passion fruit or other sorbet, softened

1 pint vanilla ice cream, slightly softened

1 quart chocolate ice cream, slightly softened

1 cup chocolate wafer cookie crumbs (about 17 crushed cookies)

1 loaf pound cake

FOR THE MERINGUE

1 cup egg whites (about 6 large), at room temperature

Pinch of cream of tartar

1 cup sugar

This cake is a guaranteed showstopper. Be sure to completely cover the ice cream with meringue—it acts as an insulator and keeps the ice cream from melting.

1 Make the ice cream cake: Brush a 3-quart metal bowl with vegetable oil; line with plastic wrap. Fill the bowl with scoops of the sorbet, vanilla ice cream and half of the chocolate ice cream, alternating small and large scoops to create a mosaic of colors and shapes. Place a piece of plastic wrap on top of the ice cream; press down to close the gaps between scoops and even out the surface. Remove the plastic wrap, sprinkle the ice cream with the cookie crumbs and re-cover with the plastic wrap, pressing gently. Freeze until set, about 30 minutes.

2 Remove the plastic and spread the remaining chocolate ice cream in an even layer on top of the crumbs. Cut the pound cake into ½-inch-thick slices; completely cover the ice cream with the slices, trimming as needed (you'll use about two-thirds of the cake). Cover with fresh plastic wrap and freeze until firm, at least 2 hours or up to 2 days.

3 Make the meringue: Whip the egg whites and cream of tartar in a large bowl with a mixer on medium-high speed until foamy, about 2 minutes. Gradually beat in the sugar on high speed until the whites are glossy and hold stiff peaks.

4 Remove the top layer of plastic wrap, then invert the cake onto a parchment-lined baking sheet. (If necessary, let the cake stand overturned until it slips out.) Remove the rest of the plastic wrap and cover the ice cream completely with the meringue, making the dome-shaped top slightly thicker than the sides. Form swirly peaks in the meringue using the back of a spoon. Freeze for at least 3 more hours.

5 Position a rack in the middle of the oven and preheat to 500°. Bake the cake until the meringue peaks are golden, about 4 minutes, or brown the meringue with a kitchen torch. Let the cake soften at room temperature for 5 to 10 minutes before slicing.

VANILLA MALTED ICE CREAM CAKE

SERVES 12

ACTIVE: 40 min

TOTAL: 4 hr 40 min

 1 12-ounce store-bought angel food cake

1½ cups cold heavy cream

 ¼ cup plus 2 tablespoons malted milk powder

 Cooking spray

1½ quarts vanilla ice cream, softened

 White sprinkles, for topping (optional)

To get the all-white look on this cake, trim the brown crust off the angel food cake. You can freeze the scraps to use as an ice cream topping another time.

1 Trim the brown crust off the top, bottom and sides of the angel food cake using a serrated knife. Thinly slice the cake.

2 Whisk ½ cup heavy cream and ¼ cup malted milk powder in a small bowl until the powder is mostly dissolved; let sit 5 minutes, then whisk again until the powder is completely dissolved and the mixture is slightly thickened. Lightly coat the bottom and sides of a 10-inch tube pan with cooking spray. Press about half of the cake slices into the bottom of the pan and slightly up the sides in a single layer, trimming as needed. Drizzle half of the malted cream over the cake slices.

3 Scoop half of the ice cream into the pan and spread with an offset spatula to make an even layer. Press some of the remaining cake slices on top of the ice cream to make an even layer, trimming the slices as needed. Drizzle with the remaining malted cream. Repeat with the remaining ice cream and cake slices. Cover with plastic wrap and freeze until firm, at least 4 hours or up to 5 days.

4 Loosen the edges of the cake with an offset spatula, then invert onto a platter. Beat the remaining 1 cup heavy cream and 2 tablespoons malted milk powder with a mixer until stiff peaks form. Spread over the top and sides of the cake and top with sprinkles.

CHOCOLATE-BANANA ICE CREAM PIE

SERVES 6 TO 8

ACTIVE: 30 min

TOTAL: 5 hr 10 min

60 vanilla wafer cookies (about three-quarters of a 12-ounce box)

1 cup unsweetened shredded coconut, plus toasted coconut for topping (optional)

1 stick unsalted butter, melted

2 medium bananas

1 pint vanilla ice cream

1 pint chocolate ice cream

1 cup cold heavy cream

2 teaspoons confectioners' sugar

The unsweetened coconut in this crust helps offset the sugary cookies and ice cream.

1 Pulse the cookies, coconut and butter in a food processor until finely ground. Press into the bottom and halfway up the sides of a 9-inch springform pan. Slice the bananas and arrange in a layer over the crust. Freeze until the crust sets, about 20 minutes. Meanwhile, let the vanilla ice cream soften at room temperature.

2 Spread the vanilla ice cream evenly over the banana layer. Freeze until firm, about 2 hours. Let the chocolate ice cream soften at room temperature, then spread over the vanilla layer. Cover with plastic wrap and freeze until firm, at least 2 hours.

3 Remove the pie from the freezer 20 minutes before serving. Beat the cream and confectioners' sugar with a mixer until soft peaks form, then spread over the pie. Top with toasted coconut.

COFFEE-COCONUT ICE CREAM BOMBE

SERVES 8

ACTIVE: 20 min

TOTAL: 3 hr

- 1½ quarts vanilla ice cream, slightly softened
- 1 quart coffee ice cream, slightly softened
- 1 10-to-12-ounce pound cake, cut lengthwise into 1-inch-thick slices
- 3 tablespoons bourbon (optional)
- 2 cups sweetened shredded coconut, toasted

To make this cake kid-friendly, use chocolate ice cream, skip the bourbon and cover the outside in crushed cereal.

1 Line a 3-quart, 9-inch-diameter bowl with plastic wrap. Scoop the vanilla ice cream into the bowl; top with a sheet of plastic wrap and gently press the ice cream into the bottom and up the sides of the bowl in an even layer, stopping about 1 inch below the rim and leaving a crater in the center. Freeze until firm, about 45 minutes.

2 Remove the plastic wrap and scoop the coffee ice cream into the vanilla ice cream crater. Pack in the ice cream and smooth the top.

3 Brush both sides of the pound cake slices with the bourbon. Press the cake slices on top of the ice cream in a single layer to cover completely, trimming as needed (you may have some cake left over). Cover with plastic wrap and freeze until firm, about 2 hours.

4 Remove the top layer of plastic wrap and invert the bowl onto a serving plate. Wipe the outside of the bowl with a hot cloth, then remove the bowl. Remove the plastic wrap and press the coconut onto the cake. Serve immediately or cover and freeze for up to 2 days.

⑤ TWISTS ON ICE CREAM SANDWICHES

SALTED CARAMEL
Spread dulce de leche on Ritz crackers. Sandwich with vanilla ice cream.

CHERRY-ALMOND
Cut almond croissants in half, then split open. Lightly toast and let cool. Sandwich with cherry-vanilla ice cream.

COFFEE
Split mini chocolate-covered doughnuts in half; sandwich with coffee ice cream.

PB&J
Break graham crackers into squares. Spread half of the squares with raspberry jam. Spread the other squares with peanut butter and black raspberry ice cream; sandwich together.

CHOCOLATE-BANANA
Sandwich mini banana bread slices with chocolate ice cream.

CHOCOLATE-HAZELNUT ICE CREAM CUPCAKES

SERVES 6

ACTIVE: 35 min

TOTAL: 1 hr 35 min

- ½ cup blanched hazelnuts, plus chopped nuts for topping
- ¾ cup packed sweetened shredded coconut
- 1 cup crispy rice cereal
- ¼ cup sweetened condensed milk

  Cooking spray
- 1 pint coconut or vanilla ice cream, slightly softened
- 2 pints chocolate ice cream

These treats come in their own edible bowls. You might need to use a little force to pry them out of the pan; if they're frozen solid, they shouldn't break.

1 Preheat the oven to 400°. Spread the whole hazelnuts and the coconut on a baking sheet and toast until deep golden, 8 to 10 minutes. Let cool, then transfer to a food processor. Add the cereal and condensed milk and pulse until the mixture is finely ground.

2 Lightly spray 6 muffin-pan cups with cooking spray. Divide the coconut-hazelnut mixture among the cups. Wet your fingers, then press the mixture into the bottom and up the sides of each cup. Freeze until firm, at least 20 minutes.

3 Remove the muffin pan from the freezer. Fill the crusts with the coconut ice cream, smoothing the tops. Freeze until firm, about 40 minutes.

4 Top each ice cream cupcake with a scoop of chocolate ice cream (make the scoop flat on the bottom, so it sits on top of the coconut ice cream). Top with the chopped hazelnuts and serve immediately. (Or cover and freeze for up to 2 days. To unmold, run an offset spatula around the edges of each cup, then pry out the cupcakes.)

SAMOA TARTLETS

MAKES 12 TARTLETS

ACTIVE: 20 min

TOTAL: 1 hr

- 3 tablespoons cold unsalted butter, cut into pieces, plus more for the pan
- ⅓ cup all-purpose flour
- 1 cup sweetened shredded coconut, toasted, plus more for topping
- 2 tablespoons packed light brown sugar
- ¼ teaspoon salt
- 5 ounces semisweet or bittersweet chocolate, finely chopped
- 1 quart coconut ice cream or sorbet
- ¾ cup dulce de leche, warmed

These treats taste like the ice cream version of one of our favorite Girl Scout cookies. You can make the crusts ahead of time, then wrap in plastic wrap and freeze for up to 1 month.

1 Preheat the oven to 350°. Butter a 12-cup muffin pan.

2 Pulse the flour, ¼ cup coconut, the brown sugar and salt in a food processor until combined. Add the cold butter and pulse until the mixture resembles wet sand with pea-size pieces, about 5 times. Put 1 heaping tablespoon of the mixture in each muffin cup and press to make even rounds. Bake until the crusts are golden, about 20 minutes.

3 Remove the pan from the oven and sprinkle the chocolate evenly over each crust. Turn off the oven; return the pan to the oven to melt the chocolate, about 3 minutes. Sprinkle each crust with 1 tablespoon of the remaining coconut. Let cool slightly, then freeze the crusts in the pan until set, about 15 minutes.

4 With a thin spatula, gently remove each crust from the muffin pan. Top with a small scoop of the coconut ice cream, drizzle with the dulce de leche and top with more coconut.

CHERRY-CHOCOLATE ICE CREAM

SERVES 6

ACTIVE: 40 min

TOTAL: 6 hr 40 min (plus churning)

- 1⅓ cups halved pitted cherries (about 13 ounces whole cherries)
- ½ cup plus 2 tablespoons sugar
- ½ cup dark rum (or water)
- 1½ cups whole milk
- 4 large egg yolks
- 3 ounces semisweet chocolate, chopped
- 1 ounce unsweetened chocolate, chopped
- 1 tablespoon unsalted butter
- ¾ cup heavy cream
- 1½ teaspoons vanilla extract

You'll need to pit a lot of cherries to make this ice cream. If you don't have a pitter, try smashing the cherries with the flat side of a chef's knife to split them open, then pull out the pits.

1 Put the cherries, 2 tablespoons sugar and the rum in a saucepan and cook over medium-high heat until syrupy, about 20 minutes. Remove from the heat and let cool, then refrigerate until cold, at least 2 hours.

2 Meanwhile, heat the milk and the remaining ½ cup sugar in a saucepan over medium-low heat, whisking to dissolve the sugar. Whisk the egg yolks in a small bowl. Gradually whisk about ½ cup of the warm milk mixture into the eggs, then whisk the egg mixture into the saucepan. Cook, stirring constantly, until the mixture coats a spoon and registers 168° on a candy thermometer, about 15 minutes. Remove from the heat; add the semisweet and unsweetened chocolate and the butter and set aside until the chocolate melts, about 5 minutes.

3 Transfer the chocolate mixture to a blender and puree until smooth. Pour into a large bowl and stir in the heavy cream and vanilla. Refrigerate until chilled, at least 2 hours or overnight.

4 Churn the chilled chocolate mixture in an ice cream maker. Strain the cherry mixture, reserving the syrup. When the ice cream is very thick, add the cherries and continue churning until incorporated. Transfer to a freezer-safe container. Drizzle in the reserved cherry syrup and swirl with a spoon. Cover and freeze until firm, at least 4 hours.

ICE CREAM SUNDAE CONES

MAKES 6 CONES

ACTIVE: 50 min

TOTAL: 4 hr

- 6 waffle cones
- 1 cup malted milk balls, plus 6 more for the cones
- 4 large chocolate-covered peanut butter cups, chopped
- 2 quarts vanilla and/or chocolate ice cream
- ¼ cup chocolate fudge sauce
- 5 ounces semisweet chocolate, chopped
- 1 ounce milk chocolate, chopped
- 6 tablespoons unsalted butter, cut into small pieces
- 1½ tablespoons corn syrup or agave syrup
- ½ cup roasted peanuts, finely chopped

We made our own chocolate shell topping for these cones (see step 4). It hardens just like the store-bought stuff.

1 Place a stainless-steel bowl in the freezer to chill, about 20 minutes. Set 6 tall glasses on a baking sheet and put a cone in each. Drop a malted milk ball into each cone.

2 Roughly chop 1 cup malted milk balls and put in the cold bowl with the peanut-butter-cup pieces and ice cream. Use a metal spoon to mash the candies into the ice cream, working quickly to keep it from melting.

3 Press 1 small scoop of the candy ice cream into each cone. Dot with a spoonful of fudge sauce and top with 2 large scoops of the candy ice cream. Freeze the cones (in the glasses) until firm, about 2 hours.

4 Meanwhile, melt the semisweet and milk chocolate with the butter and corn syrup in a heatproof bowl set over a saucepan of barely simmering water, stirring, until smooth (do not let the bowl touch the water). Remove the bowl from the saucepan and let sit until the chocolate is cool but still pourable, about 10 minutes.

5 Remove the cones from the glasses and dip the ice cream into the chocolate, swirling to coat. Sprinkle the peanuts over the chocolate; place the cones upright in the glasses and freeze until the chocolate shell is set, at least 1 hour or overnight.

MINI ICE CREAM SANDWICH CAKES

MAKES 18 MINI CAKES

ACTIVE: 45 min

TOTAL: 4 hr 10 min

- 4 tablespoons unsalted butter, plus more for the pans
- ¾ cup all-purpose flour
- 1 teaspoon baking powder
- ¼ teaspoon baking soda
- ¼ teaspoon salt
- ¾ cup unsweetened Dutch-process cocoa powder
- ½ cup packed light brown sugar
- ½ cup granulated sugar
- ½ cup brewed coffee
- ½ cup buttermilk
- 1 large egg
- 1 teaspoon vanilla extract
- 3 pints ice cream (any flavor)

You can cut these sandwiches into 1-inch squares and serve them as petit fours or stash them in the freezer for a snack.

1 Preheat the oven to 325°. Line the bottom of two 8-inch-square metal baking pans with parchment and lightly butter the paper. Sift the flour, baking powder, baking soda and salt into a bowl, then whisk to combine.

2 Melt the butter in a saucepan over medium heat. Add the cocoa powder and whisk until dissolved, about 1 minute. Transfer to a bowl and whisk in both sugars. Add the coffee, buttermilk, egg and vanilla; whisk until smooth. Whisk in the flour mixture until just combined.

3 Divide the batter between the prepared pans. Bake until a toothpick inserted into the center comes out with a few moist crumbs, 15 to 20 minutes. Let cool slightly in the pans, then invert onto a rack to cool completely. Transfer the cakes to a baking sheet lined with parchment, cover with plastic wrap and freeze until firm, about 1 hour.

4 Remove the ice cream from the freezer to soften, 10 to 20 minutes. Clean and dry the baking pans, then line each with plastic wrap, leaving a 4-inch overhang on all sides. Scoop all of the ice cream into one of the pans, packing it to make an even 1-inch-thick layer; smooth with a small offset spatula or the back of a spoon. Fold the plastic wrap over the ice cream to cover it, then freeze until solid, at least 1 hour.

5 Put 1 frozen cake in the remaining plastic-lined pan. Unwrap the ice cream layer and invert it on top of the cake; remove the plastic wrap. Cover with the remaining cake, pressing gently. Fold the plastic wrap over the cake to cover it and freeze until firm, about 1 hour.

6 To serve, unwrap the sandwich cake and cut into 9 squares. Cut each square in half.

ORANGE CREAM POPS

MAKES 8 POPS

ACTIVE: 30 min
TOTAL: 2 hr 20 min

Cooking spray
1 quart vanilla ice cream
1 quart orange sherbet

You can make these in almost any shape using cookie cutters. Just but be sure to choose simple cutters so the pops will be easy to unmold.

1 Place a baking sheet in the freezer to chill, about 20 minutes. Line the baking sheet with parchment paper and coat with cooking spray. Spray the insides of eight 3-to-4-inch cookie cutters and place on the parchment. Fill each cutter halfway with small scoops of ice cream and sherbet (about ½ cup of each), alternating to create a marbled effect. Repeat with another layer to fill the cutters. Smooth the surface of each with an offset spatula or the back of a spoon. Cover with plastic wrap and freeze 1 hour. Meanwhile, place another baking sheet in the freezer to chill, then line with parchment and coat with cooking spray.

2 Remove the cookie cutters from the freezer a few at a time, and use the plastic wrap to push the ice cream mixture out of the cutters. Insert a wooden stick halfway into the pop; smooth the surface if needed. Lay the pops on the other lined baking sheet, cover with plastic wrap and freeze until firm, about 30 more minutes.

ITALIAN ICE

MAKES 4 CUPS

ACTIVE: 10 min

TOTAL: 2 hr 40 min

- 3 cups halved strawberries or chopped pineapple
- 2 tablespoons sugar
- 2 tablespoons honey
- 1 tablespoon fresh lemon juice

1 Blend the fruit, sugar, honey and lemon juice with 2 cups ice in a food processor or blender until chunky. Add another 1 cup ice and blend until completely smooth.

2 Pour the mixture into a shallow baking dish; freeze 30 minutes. Scrape the ice with a fork until slushy, then freeze until firm, about 2 more hours. Scoop into paper cups.

Use this recipe as a guide to experiment with other flavors: Try mango, watermelon or raspberry—or blend two together.

Fun Project!
CHOCOLATE BOWLS

Dress up ice cream at a dinner party with edible chocolate bowls! They're easier than they look—you'll just need to temper the chocolate first. Using the instructions for the chocolate-dipped treats on page 126, temper 1½ pounds of semisweet chocolate. Partially inflate six balloons and dip the top of a balloon in the chocolate, twirling it to distribute. Hold the balloon upright and let dry for 1 minute, then repeat the dipping process 2 more times. Spoon a dollop of melted chocolate onto a parchment-lined baking sheet and center the balloon, bowl-side down, on the melted chocolate base. Repeat with the rest of the balloons, reheating the chocolate as needed. Refrigerate until hard, about 1 hour. Pop the balloons and peel them away. The bowls will keep in a cool, dry place for up to 3 days.

HOLIDAY DESSERTS

CONVERSATION HEARTS

**MAKES ABOUT
60 CANDIES**

ACTIVE: 1 hr
TOTAL: 1 hr (plus 24-hr drying)

- 1 ¼-ounce packet unflavored gelatin powder
- 1 tablespoon light corn syrup
- ½ teaspoon vanilla extract
- ⅛ teaspoon salt
- 2 1-pound boxes confectioners' sugar (about 8 cups), plus more for kneading
- Assorted food colorings, for tinting
- Assorted extracts (such as strawberry or almond), for flavoring (optional)
- Cooking spray
- Food-decorating pens

Make these candies with your favorite colors and flavors, then personalize them with your own notes. Look for food-decorating pens at craft stores or order them online.

1 Whisk the gelatin, corn syrup, vanilla, salt and ½ cup boiling water in the bowl of a stand mixer until the gelatin dissolves. Using the paddle attachment, beat in the confectioners' sugar on medium-low speed, 1 cup at a time, to make a stiff, sticky dough.

2 Transfer the dough to a clean surface and knead, adding more confectioners' sugar as needed (up to 1 cup), until the dough is smooth, pliable and slightly tacky, about 5 minutes.

3 Divide the dough into 4 pieces. Flatten 1 piece into a disk. (Cover the rest with plastic wrap.) Add a few drops each of food coloring and extract to the center of the dough; fold in the sides and pinch closed, then knead until the color is evenly distributed.

4 Lightly coat a large piece of parchment paper with cooking spray. Roll out the colored dough on the parchment until ⅛ to ¼ inch thick. Cut into hearts using a small cookie cutter; transfer to a parchment-lined baking sheet. Repeat with the remaining dough, using different colors and extracts. Let the hearts sit at room temperature, uncovered, until dry and hard, about 24 hours, flipping them halfway through. Write messages on the hearts using food-decorating pens.

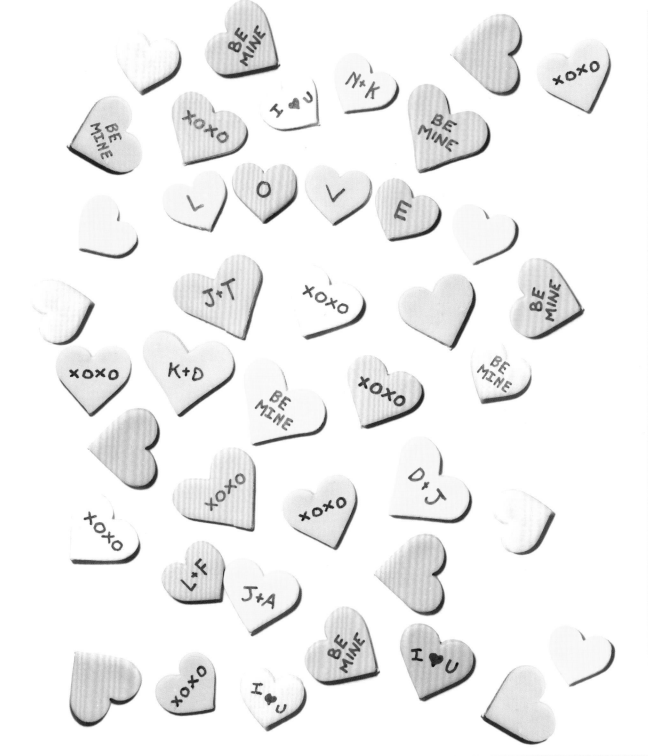

CHOCOLATE BIRDS' NESTS

MAKES 6 NESTS

ACTIVE: 20 min
TOTAL: 20 min (plus chilling)

Cooking spray

8 ounces semisweet chocolate, finely chopped

2 cups canned potato sticks

Marcona almonds, for filling

Try this sweet-salty twist on chocolate birds' nests for Easter: Use canned potato sticks instead of the usual chow mein noodles and fill with marcona almonds instead of jelly beans.

1 Coat a 6-cup muffin pan with cooking spray. Put the chocolate in a heatproof bowl and set over a saucepan of simmering water (do not let the bowl touch the water). Stir until melted and smooth.

2 Remove the bowl from the pan and stir in the potato sticks. Scoop some of the chocolate mixture into the prepared muffin-tin cups; make an indentation in each to form nests. Chill until set, at least 3 hours. Fill with marcona almonds.

KING CAKE

SERVES 10 TO 12

ACTIVE: 45 min

TOTAL: 4 hr 25 min (plus rising)

FOR THE CAKE

- ⅓ cup milk
- 1 ¼-ounce packet active dry yeast
- 2½ cups bread flour, plus more for dusting
- 2 large egg yolks plus 2 large eggs
- 3 tablespoons granulated sugar
- Grated zest of 1 lemon
- 1 teaspoon salt
- ½ teaspoon ground nutmeg
- 1½ sticks unsalted butter, melted and cooled, plus more for the bowl

FOR THE FILLING AND GLAZE

- ⅔ cup pecans, toasted
- ½ cup golden raisins
- ¼ cup bourbon
- ¾ cup packed dark brown sugar
- 1 teaspoon vanilla extract
- 1 teaspoon ground cinnamon
- 2 teaspoons grated orange zest
- ¼ teaspoon salt
- ½ cup confectioners' sugar
- Purple, green and gold sanding sugar

Make this Mardi Gras cake authentic by baking a tiny plastic baby or a dried bean inside. According to tradition, whoever finds the baby or bean is named king for a day!

1 Make the cake: Heat the milk in a saucepan over medium-low heat until scalding; transfer to a food processor, add the yeast and pulse to combine. Add ½ cup flour and the egg yolks; process to combine. Pour the remaining 2 cups flour evenly over the yeast mixture; do not process. Put the lid on; set aside for 90 minutes.

2 Add the 2 whole eggs, granulated sugar, lemon zest, salt and nutmeg to the food processor; process to make a slightly textured dough, about 1 minute. With the machine running, slowly add the melted butter to make a smooth, sticky dough. Transfer the dough to a lightly buttered bowl and cover tightly with plastic wrap; let rise in a warm place for 3 hours. Turn the dough out onto a clean surface and knead briefly; form into a ball and return to the bowl. Cover tightly with plastic wrap and refrigerate for 8 hours or overnight.

3 Make the filling: Chop the pecans. Plump the raisins in the bourbon in a small saucepan over medium heat, remove from the heat and add the brown sugar, pecans, vanilla, cinnamon, orange zest and salt. If desired, add a dried bean or plastic baby. Mix until combined.

4 On a floured surface, roll the dough into a 20-by-7-inch rectangle, with a long edge facing you. Spoon the filling in an even layer over the dough, leaving a 1-inch border along the top and bottom. Fold the bottom third and then the top third of the dough over the filling to make a tight roll; pinch to seal. Transfer the roll, seam-side down, to a parchment-lined baking sheet; tuck 1 end into the other to form a ring. Cover loosely with plastic wrap and set aside in a warm place until doubled in size, about 2 hours.

5 Preheat the oven to 350°. Bake the cake until firm and golden brown, about 40 minutes. Let cool on a rack.

6 Make the glaze: Mix 3 tablespoons water with the confectioners' sugar; brush 3 tablespoons glaze over the cake. Sprinkle with bands of colored sugar; drizzle with more glaze.

FRUIT-TART FLAG

SERVES 15 TO 20

ACTIVE: 15 min

TOTAL: 15 min

2 8-ounce containers mascarpone cheese

½ cup confectioners' sugar

½ cup chilled heavy cream

48 premade miniature tart shells or phyllo cups

Blueberries and sliced strawberry halves, for topping

These tartlets are much more fun than the usual flag cake, and you can make them in about 15 minutes. Look for mini tart shells at a gourmet store or just use mini phyllo cups.

1 Beat the mascarpone and confectioners' sugar in a large bowl with a mixer until smooth. In a separate bowl, beat the heavy cream with a mixer until soft peaks form; fold into the mascarpone mixture.

2 Fill the tart shells with the mascarpone mixture (use a piping bag, if you want), then arrange in an 8-tart-by-6-tart rectangle. Decorate the upper left-hand corner of tarts with blueberries to look like stars, then decorate the rest with strawberries to look like stripes as shown.

STAR-STUDDED BERRY TARTS

MAKES 8 TARTS

ACTIVE: 45 min
TOTAL: 3 hr 15 min

FOR THE CRUSTS

2¼ cups all-purpose flour, plus more for dusting

¾ cup pecans

6 tablespoons granulated sugar

¼ teaspoon salt

1½ sticks (12 tablespoons) cold unsalted butter, cut into ½-inch pieces

1 large egg, beaten

FOR THE PASTRY CREAM

1 cup whole milk

⅔ cup granulated sugar

1 teaspoon vanilla extract

½ cup plus 3 tablespoons buttermilk

3 large egg yolks

3 tablespoons cornstarch

1 pint raspberries

1 pint blueberries

Confectioners' sugar, for dusting

If you want to make one large tart instead, just keep the dough in one large rectangle and bake 35 to 40 minutes, removing the stars from the oven after 25 minutes.

1 Make the crusts: Pulse the flour, pecans, granulated sugar and salt in a food processor until the nuts are finely ground. Add the butter and pulse until the mixture looks like coarse meal. Drizzle in 6 tablespoons ice water and pulse until the dough comes together. Turn out onto a piece of plastic wrap and form into a disk; wrap and refrigerate until firm, about 1 hour.

2 Lightly flour a large sheet of parchment paper. Roll out the dough on the parchment into a 9-by-13-inch rectangle. Trim into an 8-by-12-inch rectangle (reserve the scraps). Cut into eight 3-by-4-inch rectangles. Separate the pieces slightly on the parchment, then use your fingers to crimp the edges. Slide the parchment onto a baking sheet. Roll out the scraps until ¼ inch thick. Cut out 8 stars using a small floured star-shaped cookie cutter; arrange on the baking sheet around the crusts. Refrigerate until firm, about 20 minutes.

3 Preheat the oven to 375°. Poke holes in the crusts with a fork. Brush the stars and the edges of the crusts with the beaten egg. Bake until golden brown, about 25 minutes; remove to a rack to cool completely.

4 Make the pastry cream: Combine the milk, ⅓ cup granulated sugar and the vanilla in a saucepan and bring to a simmer over medium heat. Whisk ½ cup buttermilk, the egg yolks, cornstarch and the remaining ⅓ cup sugar in a bowl. Slowly pour the hot milk mixture into the egg mixture, whisking constantly. Pour the mixture back into the saucepan and cook, whisking, until thick and bubbling, about 3 minutes. Transfer to a bowl; stir in the remaining 3 tablespoons buttermilk. Lay plastic wrap on the surface and refrigerate 45 minutes.

5 Carefully transfer the crusts to a platter. Spread the pastry cream on the crusts, then top with the berries. Top each tart with a star. Dust with confectioners' sugar.

GHASTLY MERINGUES

MAKES 8 TO 10 MERINGUES

ACTIVE: 35 min

TOTAL : 1 hr 35 min (plus cooling)

---

   3 large egg whites
   ½ teaspoon cream of tartar
   ¾ cup sugar
   ½ cup semisweet chocolate
      chips

These edible ghosts are just swirls of meringue. To fill your piping bag without making a mess, place it in a tall glass (tip down) and cuff the edges over the rim before filling.

1 Position a rack in the middle of the oven and preheat to 200°. Line a baking sheet with parchment paper. Beat the egg whites and cream of tartar in a large bowl with a mixer on medium speed until frothy. Beat in the sugar; increase the mixer speed to high and beat until stiff peaks form, 5 to 6 minutes.

2 Transfer the meringue to a pastry bag fitted with a large round tip. Pipe swirls of the meringue on the baking sheet and bake until dry, 1 hour to 1 hour, 15 minutes. Transfer the baking sheet to a rack and let cool completely.

3 Put the chocolate chips in a microwave-safe bowl; microwave on 50 percent power until melted, about 1 minute, stirring halfway. Transfer the melted chocolate to a resealable plastic bag and snip a corner. Pipe the chocolate on the meringues to look like eyes.

CANDY BUCKET CAKE

SERVES ABOUT 20

ACTIVE: 1 hr
TOTAL: 3 hr

Cooking spray

2 16-to-20-ounce boxes spice cake mix

8 large eggs

2 cups buttermilk

⅔ cup vegetable oil

2 16-ounce tubs vanilla frosting

Orange gel food coloring

Cornstarch, for dusting

12 ounces orange rolled fondant

½ cup dark chocolate frosting

2 long black licorice strings

Snack-size candy, for topping

To make the face on this candy bucket look-alike, draw eyes, a nose and a mouth on paper, cut them out and attach them to the fondant with toothpicks, then just cut around the outside.

1 Preheat the oven to 350°. Spray one 8-inch-round cake pan and two 6-cup Bundt pans with cooking spray. Beat the cake mixes, eggs, buttermilk and oil with a mixer; divide among the pans. Bake until a toothpick comes out clean, about 25 minutes for the round cake and 30 to 35 minutes for the Bundts; let cool.

2 Tint the vanilla frosting with orange food coloring. Trim the flat sides of the Bundt cakes and the top of the round cake to make them level. Turn one Bundt cake upside down; spread with frosting. Top with the round cake, more frosting and the other Bundt cake, then frost the whole cake and refrigerate 30 minutes.

3 Lightly dust a sheet of wax paper with cornstarch. Roll out the fondant on the paper into a 21-by-8-inch rectangle, about ⅛ inch thick. Cut into 12 strips, 8 inches long and 1¾ inches wide; trim the four corners off of each strip so the ends are tapered. Attach the fondant strips to the cake, pressing and smoothing them from the base of the cake upward. Refrigerate the cake 30 minutes.

4 Draw jack-o'-lantern eyes, a nose and a mouth on paper and cut them out; attach to the cake with toothpicks. Score around the cutouts with a paring knife, then remove the toothpicks and paper. Trace the scored lines with the knife, cutting through the fondant and slightly into the cake. Pry out the pieces with the tip of the knife.

5 Using a knife, extend the hole in the top of the cake to 4 inches wide and 1 inch deep. Put the dark chocolate frosting in a resealable plastic bag; snip a corner and pipe the frosting into the cutouts. Twist the 2 strings of licorice together and insert into the top of the cake to make a handle. Fill the top of the cake with snack-size candy.

6 TWISTS
ON
CARAMEL APPLES

MAKES 6 APPLES

ACTIVE: 30 min

TOTAL: 30 min

- 2 cups sugar
- ¼ cup light corn syrup
- ½ cup heavy cream
- 2 tablespoons unsalted butter
- 1 teaspoon vanilla extract
- Pinch of salt
- Cooking spray
- 6 apples
- Assorted toppings (optional)

Try something other than crushed peanuts on your caramel apples: We found some surprisingly great combos.

1 Mix the sugar, corn syrup and ½ cup water in a saucepan. Bring to a boil over medium-high heat, stirring just until the sugar dissolves. Cook, swirling the pan (do not stir), until the mixture is light amber and a candy thermometer registers 320°, 8 to 10 minutes.

2 Remove from the heat; slowly whisk in the heavy cream, then the butter, vanilla and salt. Return to low heat and whisk until smooth. Let cool until the caramel is thick enough to coat a spoon.

3 Line a baking sheet with parchment; coat with cooking spray. Insert lollipop sticks into the stem ends of the apples. Dip into the caramel, letting the excess drip off. Roll in toppings and let cool on the baking sheet.

CHEDDAR CRUNCH
Roll in crushed cheese crackers.

ASIAN FUSION
Roll in diced crystallized
ginger and sesame seeds

BALLPARK BLEND
Roll in salted peanuts
and caramel popcorn.

HEALTH NUT
Roll in chopped walnuts
and dried cranberries.

TROPICAL TWIST
Roll in toasted shredded coconut
and chopped macadamia nuts.

COOKIES AND CREAM
Roll in crushed Oreo cookies and
drizzle with melted white chocolate.

CANDY CORN CAKE

SERVES 10 TO 12

ACTIVE: 1 hr

TOTAL: 1 hr

1 store-bought jelly-roll cake
   or large pound cake

1 16-ounce tub vanilla
   frosting

3 9-ounce bags candy corn

4 ounces green rolled
   fondant

   Cornstarch, for dusting

To make this Halloween corn-on-the-cob cake look like Indian corn, alternate traditional candy corn with other flavors like chocolate and caramel.

1 Trim the ends of the cake to make a corn-cob shape. Cover with a thin layer of the vanilla frosting, then cover the cake completely with the candy corn, inserting the tips into the cake so that only the yellow ends are visible.

2 Roll out the green fondant on a cornstarch-dusted surface until about ⅛ inch thick. Cut out 2 leaf-shaped pieces and arrange around the cake to look like husks.

POLKA-DOT PUMPKIN PIE

SERVES 8 TO 10

ACTIVE: 45 min

TOTAL: 2 hr 35 min (plus cooling)

FOR THE DOUGH

- 2½ cups all-purpose flour, plus more for dusting
- 4 tablespoons cold vegetable shortening
- 2 teaspoons sugar
- 1 teaspoon apple cider vinegar
- ½ teaspoon salt
- 1½ sticks (12 tablespoons) cold unsalted butter, cut into small pieces
- 1 large egg, beaten

FOR THE FILLING

- 1 15-ounce can pure pumpkin
- 1¼ cups heavy cream
- ⅔ cup granulated sugar
- 2 large eggs
- 1 teaspoon ground cinnamon
- ½ teaspoon ground nutmeg
- ½ teaspoon vanilla extract
- ¼ teaspoon salt
- Coarse sugar, for sprinkling

This recipe makes 2 disks of dough, enough for 2 crusts. Use the extra dough for decorating or freeze for up to 2 months.

1 Make the dough: Pulse the flour, shortening, sugar, vinegar and salt in a food processor until it looks like fine meal. Add the butter and pulse until it is in pea-size pieces. Sprinkle in ¼ cup ice water and pulse until the dough starts coming together. Pinch the dough with your fingers; if it doesn't hold together, add up to 4 more tablespoons ice water, 1 tablespoon at a time, and pulse again.

2 Divide the dough between 2 sheets of plastic wrap and pat each into a disk. Wrap tightly and refrigerate until firm, at least 1 hour or preferably overnight.

3 Roll out 1 disk of dough into a 12-inch round on a lightly floured surface. Ease into a 9-inch pie plate and fold the overhanging dough under itself. Pierce the bottom and sides all over with a fork. Roll out the other disk of dough; cut into small circles with a cookie cutter and place on a parchment-lined plate. Refrigerate the pie crust and the circles at least 1 hour or overnight.

4 Preheat the oven to 350°. Line the crust with foil and fill with pie weights or dried beans (keep the small dough circles chilled). Transfer the pie plate to the oven and bake until the edges are golden, 20 to 25 minutes. Remove the foil and weights and continue baking until the crust is golden all over, 10 to 15 more minutes. Transfer to a rack and let cool completely.

5 Make the filling: Gently whisk the pumpkin, cream, granulated sugar, eggs, cinnamon, nutmeg, vanilla and salt (do not overmix). Pour the filling into the crust. Attach the chilled dough circles to the edge of the crust with the beaten egg. Brush the circles with more egg, sprinkle with coarse sugar and bake until the filling is set around the edges, 50 minutes to 1 hour (the middle will still jiggle slightly). Transfer to a rack; let cool completely.

HOLIDAY SUGAR COOKIES

MAKES 24 TO 36 COOKIES

ACTIVE: 1 hr 10 min
TOTAL: 3 hr 25 min

FOR THE COOKIES

 2¼ cups all-purpose flour
 ¼ teaspoon salt
 2 sticks unsalted butter, at room temperature
 ½ cup granulated sugar
 ¾ cup confectioners' sugar
 2 large egg yolks
 1 teaspoon vanilla extract
 1 teaspoon finely grated lemon zest
  Cooking spray
  Sanding sugar, for decorating (optional)

FOR THE ICING

 8 ounces white or semisweet chocolate
 1 teaspoon vegetable shortening
 1 tablespoon light corn syrup
 2 tablespoons milk
 ½ cup confectioners' sugar
 ½ teaspoon vanilla extract
  Food coloring (optional)
  Nonpareils, sanding sugar, candies, coconut and/ or melted chocolate, for decorating

To make a fun design with sanding sugar like we do here, use a potato masher, slotted spoon or spatula as a stencil.

1 Make the cookies: Combine the flour and salt in a bowl. Put the butter, granulated sugar and confectioners' sugar in the bowl of a stand mixer fitted with the paddle attachment; beat on medium speed until light and fluffy, about 4 minutes (or about 6 minutes if using a hand mixer). Add the egg yolks, one at a time, beating on medium-high speed after each addition. Add the vanilla and lemon zest and beat until combined. Add the flour mixture in 2 batches and mix until just incorporated. Divide the dough in half, wrap in plastic wrap and refrigerate at least 1 hour.

2 Line 2 baking sheets with parchment and coat with cooking spray. Roll out each piece of dough between 2 sheets of parchment until about ⅛ inch thick (return the dough to the refrigerator if it softens too much). Cut into shapes with cookie cutters; arrange 2 inches apart on the prepared baking sheets. Reroll the scraps and cut out more cookies. Sprinkle with sanding sugar, if desired. Refrigerate the cutouts 1 hour.

3 Preheat the oven to 350°. Bake the cookies until lightly golden around the edges, 12 to 15 minutes. Let cool 3 minutes on the baking sheets, then transfer to racks to cool completely.

4 Meanwhile, make the icing: Finely chop the chocolate and place in a microwave-safe bowl with the shortening, corn syrup, milk, confectioners' sugar and vanilla. Cover with plastic wrap and microwave in 30-second intervals, stirring, until smooth. Pour into separate bowls and tint with food coloring, if desired.

5 Ice and decorate the cookies; transfer to a rack and let set.

PEPPERMINT CROQUEMBOUCHE

SERVES 16

ACTIVE: 2 hr

TOTAL: 3 hr

FOR THE PASTRY PUFFS

- 6 tablespoons unsalted butter
- 1 teaspoon granulated sugar
- ¼ teaspoon salt
- 1 cup all-purpose flour
- 3 large eggs

FOR THE FILLING

- 10 ounces white chocolate, finely chopped
- ⅔ cup heavy cream
- ¼ teaspoon peppermint extract
- 1 16-ounce container mascarpone cheese

FOR ASSEMBLY

- 2½ cups confectioners' sugar, plus more for dusting
- ¼ cup whole milk, plus more if needed
- Crushed candy canes, for topping

A croquembouche is a tower of cream puffs. We used icing instead of the usual caramel to hold it together.

1 Make the puffs: Preheat the oven to 450° and line 2 baking sheets with parchment. Bring 1 cup water, the butter, granulated sugar and salt to a boil. Remove from the heat and sift the flour directly into the pan; stir with a wooden spoon to form a paste. Return to medium heat and cook, stirring constantly, until the paste is shiny and pulls away from the pan, about 3 minutes. Transfer to a stand mixer fitted with the paddle attachment and beat on medium speed to cool slightly, about 2 minutes. Beat in 1 egg, then 1 more. Whisk the third egg in a small bowl, then beat into the dough, 1 tablespoon at a time, until just smooth and tight.

2 Transfer the dough to a pastry bag fitted with a ¼-inch round tip. Pipe 1¼-inch rounds of dough onto the prepared baking sheets, about 1 inch apart; you'll have about 50. Smooth the dough peaks with a dampened finger, then bake until puffed, 10 minutes. Reduce the oven temperature to 350° and continue baking until golden, 5 more minutes. Turn off the oven but leave the puffs inside to dry, 5 to 7 more minutes. Remove from the oven and pierce a small hole in each puff with a paring knife to let steam escape; transfer to a rack to cool completely.

3 Make the filling: Put the white chocolate in a heatproof bowl. Bring the heavy cream to a boil, then pour it over the chocolate. Whisk until smooth and cool, about 7 minutes; whisk in the peppermint extract. Stir in the mascarpone. Cover and refrigerate until thick enough to pipe, 30 minutes. Transfer to a pastry bag fitted with a ¼-inch round tip. Insert the pastry bag tip into the hole in each puff and pipe in the filling. Transfer to a baking sheet; refrigerate 30 minutes or up to 2 hours.

4 Assemble the croquembouche: Whisk the confectioners' sugar and milk until smooth. Dip the bottom of a puff into the icing; let the excess drip off. Transfer the puff to a platter, icing-side down. Repeat with more puffs, arranging them in a 7-inch circle. Fill in the circle with more puffs to form the base. Continue building a conical tower, using icing to hold the puffs in place. (If the icing gets thick, whisk in milk 1 teaspoon at a time.) Dust the croquembouche with confectioners' sugar and sprinkle with crushed candy canes; chill until set, about 15 minutes.

CANDY CANE PAVLOVA

SERVES 8 TO 10

ACTIVE: 1 hr
TOTAL: 2 hr (plus cooling)

2 pints vanilla ice cream

1 teaspoon peppermint extract

¼ cup crushed candy canes, plus more for topping

4 large egg whites

1¼ cups superfine sugar

Pinch of salt

Red food coloring

We filled this red-and-white meringue shell with peppermint ice cream: You can flavor vanilla ice cream like we did, or look for limited-edition peppermint ice cream around the holidays.

1 Prepare the ice cream: Let the ice cream soften slightly at room temperature, 5 minutes. Transfer to a stand mixer fitted with the paddle attachment and beat until creamy but not melted, about 1 minute. Add ½ teaspoon peppermint extract and the crushed candy canes and beat until just incorporated, about 30 seconds. Transfer to a small metal baking dish or loaf pan, cover and freeze until firm, 1 to 2 hours.

2 Meanwhile, preheat the oven to 300° and line a baking sheet with parchment paper. Using a bowl or cake pan as a guide, trace an 8-inch circle onto the parchment with a pencil, then flip the parchment over (the circle should still be visible); set aside.

3 Make the meringue: Fill a medium saucepan with 1 to 2 inches of water and bring to a simmer over medium-high heat; remove from the heat. Combine the egg whites, sugar and salt in a large heatproof bowl and set over the hot water (do not let the bowl touch the water). Whisk until the egg whites are foamy and hot, about 5 minutes. Remove the bowl from the pan and beat with a mixer on medium speed until stiff and shiny, about 10 minutes. Beat in the remaining ½ teaspoon peppermint extract until combined.

4 Transfer the meringue to a pastry bag fitted with a ½-inch round tip. Pipe in a tight spiral onto the prepared parchment-lined baking sheet, starting in the middle of the circle and working toward the outer edge. Pipe more meringue around the outer edge of the circle to build up the side about 2 inches high. Dip a small paintbrush or toothpick in the food coloring, then drag it around the meringue spiral to create streaks. Repeat several times.

5 Bake until the meringue is just firm but not brown, about 1 hour. (If it starts browning, reduce the oven temperature to 275°.) Transfer to a rack and let cool completely. (The meringue will continue to harden as it cools.) Carefully invert the meringue onto a platter and gently peel off the parchment. Invert again and set on the platter. Top with scoops of the prepared peppermint ice cream and sprinkle with more crushed candy canes. Freeze until ready to serve, up to 2 days.

GINGERBREAD PEOPLE

MAKES 24 TO 36 COOKIES

ACTIVE: 1 hr
TOTAL: 3 hr 30 min

FOR THE COOKIES

3½ cups all-purpose flour, plus
more for dusting

1 teaspoon baking soda

1 teaspoon salt

1 tablespoon ground ginger

2 teaspoons ground
cinnamon

¼ teaspoon ground cloves

¼ teaspoon ground allspice

6 tablespoons unsalted
butter, melted

1 tablespoon vegetable
shortening, melted

⅔ cup packed light brown
sugar

¾ cup molasses

1 large egg

FOR THE ROYAL ICING

2 tablespoons meringue
powder

1 pound confectioners' sugar
(about 4 cups)

Assorted candies, for
decorating (see pages
320-21)

Royal icing hardens completely when it dries, so it's great
for cookie decorating. To fill or "flood" the cookies with icing,
draw the outlines first, then thin the icing a bit with water and
spread it inside the lines with a paintbrush.

1 Make the cookies: Sift the flour, baking soda, salt, ginger, cinnamon,
cloves and allspice into a large bowl. In another large bowl, combine
the butter, shortening, brown sugar and molasses; add the egg and beat
with a mixer until combined. Beat in the flour mixture in 2 additions.
Divide the dough in half; wrap each half in plastic and pat into a ½-inch
thickness. Refrigerate 2 hours.

2 Preheat the oven to 350°. Line 2 baking sheets with parchment paper.
On a floured surface, roll out each piece of dough until ¼ inch thick,
dusting with flour, if needed. Using 3-to-5-inch cookie cutters, cut out
gingerbread people and arrange 1 inch apart on the prepared baking
sheets. Brush off the excess flour and refrigerate 15 minutes.

3 Bake until the cookies are golden around the edges, 10 to 12 minutes.
Transfer to racks to cool completely.

4 Make the icing: Sift the meringue powder and confectioners' sugar
into a large bowl. Beat in 6 tablespoons water with a mixer until the
icing is glossy with soft peaks. Transfer to a resealable plastic bag; snip
the tip off a corner. Pipe onto the cookies and decorate with candies.

MINI MARSHMALLOW DUO
Snip mini marshmallows in half with scissors; toss in colored sugar (it sticks to the cut sides). Attach with royal icing.

GUMDROP DUO
Smash gumdrops together and roll into sheets with a rolling pin, then cut into outfits. Attach with royal icing.

FRUIT LEATHER DUO
Cut fruit leather into pants and dresses and attach with royal icing. Use thinned icing to make a shirt.

M&M'S DUO
Use royal icing to attach M&M's to the boy and girl; alternate small and large candies to change the design.

SOUR BELT DUO
Cut sour belts into strips and squares to make shorts or a layered dress. Attach the pieces with royal icing.

JELLY BEAN DUO
Draw an outline of a suit or dress with royal icing, then thin the icing to fill it in. Attach jelly beans with more icing.

MINT DUO
Outline the cookies with royal icing, then attach peppermint candies and M&M's with icing for buttons.

NONPAREILS DUO
Attach small and large nonpareils with royal icing; line the dress or shorts with colored mini chocolate chips.

FRUIT CHEW DUO
Smash same-color fruit chews together, roll into sheets, cut holes and fill with another color. Cut out the outfits; attach with royal icing.

STAINED GLASS DUO
Cut shapes out of the people before baking. Bake, then fill the holes with crushed hard candies; return to the oven and bake until melted.

HOT COCOA COOKIES

MAKES ABOUT 15 COOKIES

ACTIVE: 45 min

TOTAL: 2 hr 45 min

- 2¼ cups cake flour, plus more for dusting
- ¼ cup unsweetened Dutch-process cocoa powder
- 1 teaspoon baking soda
- ¼ teaspoon salt
- 2 sticks unsalted butter, at room temperature
- ¾ cup sugar
- 1 large egg
- 1 teaspoon vanilla extract
- ½ cup marshmallow cream

Store-bought marshmallow cream makes a great sandwich-cookie filling. It tends to ooze as it sits, though, so don't spread it all the way to the edges.

1 Sift the flour, cocoa powder, baking soda and salt into a medium bowl.

2 Beat the butter and sugar in a large bowl with a mixer on medium-high speed until light and fluffy, 3 to 5 minutes. Add the egg and vanilla and beat until incorporated. Reduce the mixer speed to low; add the flour mixture in 2 batches and beat until just incorporated. Divide the dough in half, wrap in plastic wrap and refrigerate until firm, at least 1 hour and up to 1 day.

3 Line 2 baking sheets with parchment paper. Working with 1 piece of dough at a time, dust the dough generously with flour and roll out between 2 pieces of parchment paper until ⅛ inch thick. Cut out shapes using 2-to-4-inch cookie cutters and transfer to the prepared baking sheets. Gather the scraps and refrigerate until firm; reroll once to cut out more cookies. Refrigerate the cutouts until firm, about 30 minutes.

4 Position racks in the upper and lower thirds of the oven and preheat to 350°. Bake the cookies, switching the pans halfway through, until slightly puffed and darker around the edges, 12 to 15 minutes. Let cool 5 minutes on the baking sheets, then transfer to racks to cool completely. Sandwich the cookies with the marshmallow cream.

COCOA THUMBPRINTS

MAKES ABOUT 36 COOKIES

ACTIVE: 30 min
TOTAL: 1 hr 15 min

- 1½ cups all-purpose flour
- ¾ cup granulated sugar, plus ½ cup for rolling
- ½ cup unsweetened Dutch-process cocoa powder
- 1 teaspoon baking powder
- ½ teaspoon salt
- 6 tablespoons unsalted butter, melted
- 2 large eggs, lightly beaten
- ½ cup confectioners' sugar
- Sprinkles, mini marshmallows, mini candies or candied cherries, for filling

We like using Dutch-process cocoa powder for these thumbprints: It gives them a darker color and deeper flavor.

1 Whisk the flour, ¾ cup granulated sugar, the cocoa powder, baking powder and salt in a bowl. Add the melted butter and eggs and stir until combined. Cover and refrigerate the dough until firm, about 30 minutes.

2 Preheat the oven to 325°. Line 2 baking sheets with parchment. Place the confectioners' sugar and the remaining ½ cup granulated sugar in 2 separate small bowls. Roll scant tablespoonfuls of the dough into balls; roll in the granulated sugar and then in the confectioners' sugar. Place 1 inch apart on the prepared baking sheets. Lightly flatten each ball with your fingers and make a deep ½-inch-wide indentation in the center with your thumb. Place your choice of filling in the indentation.

3 Bake until the cookies are puffed and slightly cracked, about 10 minutes. Let cool 3 minutes on the baking sheets; transfer to racks to cool completely.

GERMAN CHOCOLATE YULE LOG

SERVES 8 TO 12

ACTIVE: 45 min

TOTAL: 1 hr 15 min

Vegetable oil, for brushing

1¼ cups all-purpose flour, plus more for dusting

1 cup evaporated milk

2¼ cups granulated sugar

3 large egg yolks plus 3 large eggs, at room temperature

2½ sticks unsalted butter (1 stick cubed, 1½ sticks softened)

3 teaspoons vanilla extract

1⅔ cups sweetened shredded coconut, toasted

1 cup chopped pecans

½ teaspoon baking soda

½ teaspoon salt

¼ cup unsweetened cocoa powder, plus more for dusting

1 ounce bittersweet chocolate, finely chopped

⅓ cup hot strong coffee

⅓ cup buttermilk

Confectioners' sugar, for dusting

When you make a roulade, be sure to roll up the cake while it's still slightly warm. The cake will be less likely to crack.

1 Preheat the oven to 350°. Lightly brush a 13-by-18-inch jelly-roll pan with vegetable oil; line with parchment paper, letting it come up the short sides by about 2 inches. Brush the paper with oil and lightly dust with flour.

2 For the filling, whisk the evaporated milk, 1 cup granulated sugar, 3 egg yolks and the cubed butter in a saucepan over medium heat. Cook, stirring constantly, until thick and creamy, about 10 minutes. Remove from the heat; stir in 1 teaspoon vanilla, the coconut and pecans. Set aside to cool completely, stirring occasionally.

3 Meanwhile, whisk the flour, baking soda and salt in a medium bowl. Whisk the cocoa and chocolate in another bowl. Add the hot coffee to the cocoa mixture, stirring until smooth; stir in the buttermilk and the remaining 2 teaspoons vanilla.

4 Using a mixer, beat the softened butter and the remaining 1¼ cups granulated sugar in a large bowl on high speed until fluffy, about 4 minutes. Reduce the speed to low; add the 3 whole eggs, one at a time, incorporating each before adding the next. Add the flour mixture in 3 parts, alternating with the cocoa mixture in 2 parts, beginning and ending with the flour. Beat until just blended; if necessary, fold the batter together with a rubber spatula.

5 Spread the batter evenly in the prepared pan. Bake until the cake springs back when pressed lightly, about 16 minutes. Let cool slightly in the pan.

6 Run a knife around the edges and slide the cake with its paper onto a work surface. Spread the coconut filling evenly over the cake. Roll the cake from 1 of the short ends, pulling it away from the parchment into a tight cylinder; transfer to a platter. Let cool completely and dust with confectioners' sugar or cocoa.

Fun Project!
EDIBLE TREES

Gather some friends for an edible tree-trimming party before the holidays: These sweet
miniature trees are super easy to make. Just stick sour tape, gummy spearmint leaves and
gummy dots into foam cones with toothpicks. Make sure you keep some extra candy around
for repairs, in case someone plucks off a piece or two as a snack!

1 For a sour-tape tree: Cut the candy into 1-inch pieces. You'll need 2 pounds of candy for a 12-inch foam cone.

2 Cut about 260 toothpicks in half. Using a wine cork, push the toothpicks through the tops of the sour tape into the foam, working in a circle.

3 Keep adding layers of sour tape, overlapping them so that each new layer covers the toothpicks below. Cover the tip of the tree with 1 piece of sour tape.

1 For a gummy dot tree: Cut about 350 toothpicks in half, and cut the top third off about 150 more. For a spearmint leaf tree: Cut about 220 toothpicks in half.

2 Attach a green gummy dot or spearmint leaf to each toothpick. Starting at the base, push candies into the tree (use shorter toothpicks at the top). You'll need about 2 pounds of candy for an 8-inch foam cone.

3 Swap some gummy dots for colored ones to make "lights."

INDEX

PHOTOGRAPHY CREDITS

Main cover photograph by Kana Okada

Back cover photograph by Jonathan Kantor

ANTONIS ACHILLEOS: pages 140, 150-151, 172, 180-181, 186-187

LEVI BROWN: pages 43, 87, 93-96, 101, 126-128, 135, 165-166, 190-191, 200-201, 204, 223, 227, 235, 243, 250-252, 259, 283-288, 309, 330

GEMMA COMMAS: pages 328-329

TARA DONNE: page 298

STEPHANIE FOLEY: pages 32, 84, 228

STEVE GIRALT: pages 74, 211, 261, 267, 313, 318-321, 324

CHRISTINA HOLMES: page 88

RAYMOND HOM: page 302

KARL JUENGEL/STUDIO D: pages 306-307

JONATHAN KANTOR: pages 112, 274-275

SAM KAPLAN: pages 20, 26, 58-59, 293-294

KANG KIM: pages 29, 53, 99, 119, 121, 123, 174-175, 184-185

YUNHEE KIM: pages 80-81, 117, 148, 255

DAVID MALOSH: page 24

CHARLES MASTERS: pages 51, 118, 170-171, 247

KATE MATHIS: pages 57, 108

ELLIE MILLER: page 327

JOHNNY MILLER: pages 60, 65, 78-79, 92, 102, 132, 139, 216, 231, 239, 244, 248, 268, 290, 310, 314, 317, 323

MARCUS NILSSON: page 208

KANA OKADA: pages 66, 77, 162, 207, 212, 240, 256, 262, 265, 272, 276

CON POULOS: pages 23, 31, 35, 36, 39, 44-48, 54, 70, 83, 131, 147, 154, 157, 161, 215, 219, 232, 236, 271, 301

ANDREW PURCELL: pages 40, 153, 176-177, 280

LARA ROBBY/STUDIO D: page 297

TINA RUPP: page 279

KATE SEARS: page 90

LISA SHIN: pages 73, 124, 158, 194-199, 202-203

KAT TEUTSCH: pages 136, 143-144, 178-179, 182-183, 188-189, 192-193, 305

JUSTIN WALKER: page 111

ANNA WILLIAMS: pages 62, 169, 220, 224

JAMES WOJCIK: pages 69, 97, 105-107, 115, 289